the Country Table
Classic recipes from a country kitchen

foreword

Over forty years ago I left the comfort of the city to follow my man to the back of beyond. From compulsory Invalid Cooking Classes during my nursing training, I was suddenly thrust into the reality of bush cooking in my new home – a camp on the banks of a dry creek bed. There was no kitchen let alone recipe books and the nearest shops were 600 kilometres away. Those early beginnings instilled in me the ability to serve nourishing food despite limited resources and ingredients.

Riveren, our remote outback cattle station home, sprawls over 3,000 square kilometres and supports 20,000 Brahman cattle. Our children initially established extensive vegetable gardens and orchards. Today we still epitomise 'homegrown' in every sense of the word. My regular table guests are my family and members of our multi-skilled workforce. Numbers swell when we open our doors to passing travellers – including road train drivers, flying padres, mobile health sisters, livestock agents – and friends from afar. For all of us, every meal is a feast, a celebration and an occasion – to share stories and experiences, to review today and plan tomorrow.

In our ever-changing world where global warming and climate change infiltrate dinner conversations, the issue of food safety has never been more important. We Australian farmers understand the need to retain our worldwide reputation as producers of clean green food. And consumers these days will accept nothing less.

Timely indeed is this magnificent book of classic recipes to be readily embraced by one and all irrespective of location and lifestyle. I'm sure this recipe collection will resonate loudly with you all, to unite country and city around *The Country Table*.

Terry Underwood OAM, Riveren Station, Northern Territory.

introduction

contents

INTRODUCTION 8

A HEARTY BREAKFAST 10

A CUPPA ON THE VERANDAH 32

LET'S EAT OUTDOORS 58

FEEDING THE SHEARERS 86

SUNDAY LUNCH 88

SEE YOU AT THREE 116

BEST IN SHOW 142

WINTER BY THE FIRE 144

THE JAM PAN 178

GLOSSARY 194

INDEX 196

CONVERSION CHART 199

welcome

This book celebrates good food and the role it plays in the daily rituals of our lives. It celebrates an approach to cooking – and a way of eating – that revolves around a close connection to fresh produce, the enjoyment of a shared table and a respect for meal times.

The term 'country-style cooking' is commonly used to describe food that is wholesome and hearty – and it is definitely those things. But it is also about an attitude. It is about being wise and creative with ingredients and it is about sharing food and honouring simple traditions like a Sunday family lunch or the happy pleasure of home-baked treats for afternoon tea.

Ingenuity is a recurring theme in Australian history and it is a key ingredient in country cooking, too. Traditionally, country cooks needed to be resourceful and innovative to make the most of their limited access to ingredients. The food they prepared relied on whatever fresh produce was available at their doorsteps and it required a thoughtful approach to ingredients: all edible parts were used in the cooking and very little was wasted.

Country cooks traditionally also were very generous in the meals they provided. They often found themselves catering for large numbers – they had bigger families, they often hosted farm workers or visitors from the city – and so the food they cooked needed to be plentiful and hearty.

All these historical elements help to define country cooking today: it is food that is produce-driven, generous and nourishing. It is based on full flavours and treasured recipes. And it is food for sharing. In the words of one of Australia's best-known country chefs, Stefano di Pieri, country cooking is about the "spirit" of the cooking.

"There isn't a type of food that is typically 'country' food. I think country cooking refers more to the spirit and the intention that goes into the cooking," he says.

"And it's about using the food of place. I think the key words associated with country cooking are generosity and rusticity or simplicity. Not that the food is simple. In fact, the food can be quite sophisticated but the presentation is simple. It's about sharing the table with family and friends and eating together with no formality."

This book takes you on a culinary and visual journey centred on dependably delicious food. Accompanied by inspirational quotes from Stefano di Pieri, Maggie Beer and *The Australian Women's Weekly*'s Test Kitchen Director, Pamela Clark – and other country cooks from around Australia – the recipes in this book speak of country hospitality and fond memories. We hope you enjoy the conviviality of *The Country Table*.

introduction

a hearty breakfast

Muesli, eggs, bacon, muffins and all the other perfect ingredients for a good start to the day.

PORRIDGE

3½ cups (875ml) hot water
1½ cups (135g) rolled oats
½ cup (125ml) milk
2 tablespoons caster sugar
1 teaspoon ground cinnamon

1 Combine the water and oats in medium saucepan over medium heat; cook, stirring, about 5 minutes or until porridge is thick and creamy.
2 Stir in milk. Serve sprinkled with combined sugar and cinnamon.

prep and cook time 10 minutes
serves 4
nutritional count per serving 4.1g total fat (1.3g saturated fat); 782kJ (187 cal); 31.4g carbohydrate; 4.7g protein; 2.4g fibre

BIRCHER MUESLI

2 cups (180g) rolled oats
1¼ cups (310ml) apple juice
1 cup (280g) natural yogurt
2 medium green-skinned apples (300g)
¼ cup (35g) roasted slivered almonds
¼ cup (40g) dried currants
¼ cup (20g) toasted shredded coconut
1 teaspoon ground cinnamon
½ cup (140g) yogurt, extra

1 Combine oats, juice and yogurt in medium bowl. Cover; refrigerate overnight.
2 Peel, core and coarsely grate one apple; stir into oat mixture with nuts, currants, coconut and cinnamon.
3 Core and thinly slice remaining apple. Serve muesli topped with extra yogurt and apple slices.

prep time 10 minutes (plus refrigeration)
serves 6
nutritional count per serving 9.2g total fat (3g saturated fat); 1120kJ (268 cal); 36.1g carbohydrate; 8.1g protein; 3.9g fibre

ROASTED MUESLI WITH DRIED FRUIT AND HONEY

2 cups (180g) rolled oats
1 cup (110g) rolled rice
¼ cup (15g) unprocessed wheat bran
¼ cup (50g) pepitas
1 teaspoon ground cinnamon
⅓ cup (115g) honey
1 tablespoon vegetable oil
¾ cup (35g) flaked coconut
⅓ cup (50g) coarsely chopped dried apricots
⅓ cup (20g) coarsely chopped dried apples
⅓ cup (55g) sultanas
¼ cup (35g) dried cranberries, chopped coarsely

1 Preheat oven to 180°C/160°C fan-forced.
2 Combine oats and rice in large bowl, then spread evenly between two oven trays. Roast, uncovered, in oven 5 minutes.
3 Stir bran, pepitas and cinnamon into oat mixtures, then drizzle evenly with combined honey and oil; stir to combine. Roast, uncovered, 5 minutes. Stir in coconut. Roast, uncovered, 5 minutes.
4 Remove trays from oven; place muesli mixture in same large bowl, stir in remaining ingredients. Serve with milk or yogurt.

prep and cook time 30 minutes
serves 6
nutritional count per serving 16.1g total fat (4.8g saturated); 1768kJ (423 cal); 52.8g carbohydrate; 7.3g protein; 11.1g fibre

TIP YOU CAN STORE THIS ROASTED MUESLI IN AN AIRTIGHT CONTAINER, IN A COOL PLACE, FOR UP TO TWO WEEKS.

TOP RIGHT BIRCHER MUESLI WITH APPLE SLICES
LEFT ROASTED MUESLI WITH DRIED FRUIT AND HONEY

15

a *hearty* breakfast

"We love a leisurely weekend breakfast at our place. We have our own chooks so we have fresh eggs with traditionally cured bacon and our own home-made marmalade."

– Maggie Beer

FRENCH TOAST

3 eggs, beaten lightly
⅓ cup (80ml) cream
⅓ cup (80ml) milk
¼ teaspoon ground cinnamon
1 tablespoon caster sugar
12 x 2cm slices french bread stick
50g butter

1 Combine egg, cream, milk, cinnamon and sugar in large bowl. Dip bread slices into egg mixture.
2 Melt half of the butter in large frying pan; cook half of the bread slices until browned both sides. Repeat with remaining butter and bread.
3 Serve french toast sprinkled with sifted icing sugar, if desired.

prep and cook time 15 minutes
serves 4
nutritional count per serving 24.8g total fat (14.3g saturated fat); 1450kJ (347 cal); 22.2g carbohydrate; 8.8g protein; 1.1g fibre

PANCAKES WITH LEMON AND SUGAR

2 cups (300g) plain flour
4 eggs, beaten lightly
2 cups (500ml) milk, approximately
40g butter
¼ cup (60ml) lemon juice, approximately
2 tablespoons sugar, approximately

1 Place flour in medium bowl. Make well in centre; gradually whisk or stir in egg and enough of the milk to make a thin, smooth batter.
2 Heat large frying pan over high heat a few minutes. Place ½ teaspoon butter in pan; swirl around pan until greased all over. Pour ¼ cup of the batter from jug into centre of pan; quickly tilt pan so that batter runs from centre around edge.
3 When pancake is browned lightly underneath, turn and brown other side. This can be done using spatula or egg slide, or pancake can be tossed and flipped over back into the pan; this takes a little practice.
4 Serve pancakes, as they are made, on warm plates; spread one side with a little of the butter. Drizzle with juice; sprinkle with sugar.

prep and cook time 25 minutes
serves 4
nutritional count per pancake 19.3g total fat (10.4g saturated fat); 2245kJ (537 cal); 69.7g carbohydrate; 19.2g protein; 2.9g fibre

> "We have eggs from the chookhouse and home-made bread which smells amazing fresh out of the oven."
> – Fiona Slack-Smith, Mudgee, New South Wales

RIGHT FRENCH TOAST
BELOW PANCAKES WITH LEMON AND SUGAR

a *hearty* breakfast

ABOVE ZUCCHINI AND MUSHROOM OMELETTE
LEFT SAUTEED MUSHROOMS

ZUCCHINI AND MUSHROOM OMELETTE

10g butter

1 clove garlic, crushed

25g button mushrooms, sliced thinly

¼ cup (50g) coarsely grated zucchini

1 green onion, chopped finely

2 eggs

1 tablespoon water

¼ cup (30g) coarsely grated cheddar cheese

1 Heat half of the butter in small frying pan; cook garlic and mushroom, stirring, over medium heat about 2 minutes or until mushroom is lightly browned. Add zucchini and onion; cook, stirring, about 1 minute or until zucchini begins to soften. Remove vegetable mixture from pan; cover to keep warm.
2 Beat eggs and the water in small bowl. Add cheese; whisk until combined.
3 Heat remaining butter in same pan; swirl pan so butter covers base. Pour egg mixture into pan; cook, tilting pan, over medium heat until almost set.
4 Place vegetable mixture evenly over half of the omelette; using spatula, flip other half over vegetable mixture. Using spatula, slide omelette gently onto serving plate.

prep and cook time 20 minutes
serves 1
nutritional count per serving 11.7g total fat (6.1g saturated fat); 606kJ (145 cal); 0.8g carbohydrate; 8.9g protein; 0.9g fibre

SAUTEED MUSHROOMS

50g butter, chopped

1 small brown onion (80g), chopped finely

500g button mushrooms, halved

1 tablespoon malt vinegar

⅓ cup coarsely chopped fresh chives

1 Melt butter in large frying pan; cook onion, stirring, until soft.
2 Add mushrooms; cook, stirring occasionally, 10 minutes or until mushrooms are tender. Add vinegar; bring to the boil. Remove from heat; stir in chives.
3 Serve mushrooms on thick toast, if desired.

prep and cook time 30 minutes
serves 4
nutritional count per serving 10.7g total fat (6.8g saturated fat); 531kJ (127 cal); 1.7g carbohydrate; 4.9g protein; 3.5g fibre

22

the *country* table

SUNDAY FRY-UP

50g butter

300g button mushrooms, sliced thickly

8 chipolata sausages (240g)

4 rashers bacon (280g)

1 tablespoon olive oil

2 medium tomatoes (190g), halved

4 eggs

1 Melt butter in medium saucepan; cook mushrooms, stirring, for 5 minutes or until tender.
2 Meanwhile, cook sausages and bacon in heated oiled large frying pan until bacon is crisp and sausages are cooked through. Remove from pan; cover to keep warm. Drain fat from pan.
3 Preheat grill.
4 Place tomato halves, cut-side up, onto baking tray. Cook under grill until browned lightly and tender.
5 Meanwhile, heat oil in same uncleaned frying pan. Break eggs into pan; cook until egg white has set and yolk is cooked as desired.
6 Serve mushrooms, sausages, bacon, tomato and eggs with thick toast, if desired.

prep and cook time 30 minutes
serves 4
nutritional count per serving 41.3g total fat (16.9g saturated fat); 2203kJ (527 cal); 4.4g carbohydrate; 34g protein; 3.2g fibre

ABOVE SCRAMBLED EGGS
LEFT FACE AT THE WINDOW

24

the *country* table

SCRAMBLED EGGS

250g cherry tomatoes

1 tablespoon olive oil

8 slices thin bacon (240g)

8 eggs

½ cup (125ml) cream

2 tablespoons finely chopped fresh chives

30g butter

4 slices crusty bread, toasted

1 Preheat grill.
2 Toss tomatoes in oil. Cook bacon and tomato under grill until bacon is crisp and tomato skins start to split. Cover to keep warm.
3 Meanwhile, combine eggs, cream and chives in medium bowl; beat lightly with fork.
4 Heat butter in large frying pan over medium heat. Add egg mixture, wait a few seconds, then use a wide spatula to gently scrape the set egg mixture along the base of the pan; cook until creamy and just set.
5 Serve toast topped with egg, bacon and tomatoes.

prep and cook time 25 minutes
serves 4
nutritional count per serving 52g total fat (23.9g saturated fat); 3223kJ (771 cal); 40g carbohydrate; 37.6g protein; 2.5g fibre

FACE AT THE WINDOW (EGG IN TOAST)

4 thick slices white bread

25g butter

4 eggs

2 tablespoons spicy tomato chutney (see page 190)

1 Cut a 7cm circle from the centre of each slice of bread. Discard centre pieces.
2 Melt butter in large frying pan; cook bread until browned lightly on one side. Turn bread; crack one egg into the centre of each piece of bread.
3 Cook, over low heat, until egg white just sets. Using spatula, gently lift toast onto serving plates. Serve with chutney.

prep and cook time 15 minutes
serves 4
nutritional count per serving 11.5g total fat (5.1g saturated fat); 1007kJ (241 cal); 23.5g carbohydrate; 10.1g protein; 1.4g fibre

a *hearty* breakfast

"Mornings on the farm meant rising early – even before the roosters – to help my nan light the wood stove and start baking for the shearers' morning tea."

– Cathie Lonnie, Corowa, New South Wales

a *hearty* breakfast

OVERNIGHT DATE AND MUESLI MUFFINS

1¼ cups (185g) plain flour

1¼ cups (160g) toasted muesli

1 teaspoon ground cinnamon

1 teaspoon bicarbonate of soda

½ cup (110g) firmly packed brown sugar

½ cup (30g) unprocessed bran

¾ cup (120g) coarsely chopped seedless dates

1½ cups (375ml) buttermilk

½ cup (125ml) vegetable oil

1 egg, beaten lightly

1 Combine ingredients in large bowl, stir until just combined. Cover; refrigerate overnight.
2 Preheat oven to 180°C/160°C fan-forced. Grease 12-hole (⅓-cup/80ml) muffin pan.
3 Divide mixture among pan holes.
4 Bake muffins about 20 minutes. Stand in pan 5 minutes; turn, top-side up, onto wire rack to cool.

prep and cook time 30 minutes (plus refrigeration)
makes 12
nutritional count per muffin 11.9g total fat (2.1g saturated fat); 1204kJ (288 cal); 38g carbohydrate; 5.4g protein; 3.7g fibre

BERRY MUFFINS

2½ cups (375g) self-raising flour

90g cold butter, chopped

1 cup (220g) caster sugar

1¼ cups (310ml) buttermilk

1 egg, beaten lightly

200g fresh or frozen mixed berries

1 Preheat oven to 180°C/160°C fan forced. Grease 12-hole (⅓-cup/80ml) muffin pan.
2 Sift flour into large bowl; rub in butter. Stir in sugar, buttermilk and egg. Do not over-mix; mixture should be lumpy. Add berries; stir through gently. Spoon mixture into pan holes.
3 Bake muffins about 20 minutes. Stand in pan 5 minutes; turn, top-side up, onto wire rack to cool.

prep and cook time 30 minutes
makes 12
nutritional count per muffin 7.5g total fat (4.6g saturated fat); 1095kJ (262 cal); 42.4g carbohydrate; 5.1g protein; 1.6g fibre

"For families on the land, the days can be long and physically demanding, so breakfast really is an important meal."
— Robyn Blanchett, Wagin, Western Australia

RIGHT OVERNIGHT DATE AND MUESLI MUFFINS
BELOW BERRY MUFFINS

a *hearty* breakfast

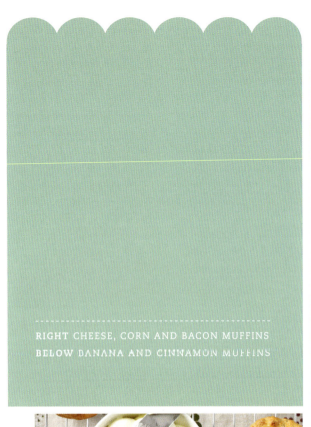

RIGHT CHEESE, CORN AND BACON MUFFINS
BELOW BANANA AND CINNAMON MUFFINS

CHEESE, CORN AND BACON MUFFINS

½ cup (85g) polenta
½ cup (125ml) milk
3 bacon rashers (210g), rind removed, chopped finely
4 green onions, chopped finely
1½ cups (225g) self-raising flour
1 tablespoon caster sugar
310g can corn kernels, drained
125g can creamed corn
100g butter, melted
2 eggs, beaten lightly
50g piece cheddar cheese
¼ cup (30g) coarsely grated cheddar cheese

1 Preheat oven to 180°C/160°C fan-forced. Oil 12-hole (⅓-cup/80ml) muffin pan.
2 Mix polenta and milk in small bowl, cover; stand 20 minutes.
3 Meanwhile, cook bacon, stirring, in heated small frying pan for 2 minutes. Add onion to pan; cook, stirring, for another 2 minutes. Remove pan from heat; cool 5 minutes.
4 Sift flour and sugar into large bowl; stir in corn kernels, creamed corn and bacon mixture. Add melted butter, eggs and polenta mixture; mix muffin batter only until just combined.
5 Spoon 1 tablespoon of the batter into each hole of muffin pan. Cut piece of cheese into 12 equal pieces; place one piece in the centre of each muffin pan hole. Divide remaining batter among pan holes; sprinkle grated cheese over each.
6 Bake muffins about 20 minutes. Turn onto wire rack. Serve muffins warm.

prep and cook time 45 minutes (plus standing time)
makes 12
nutritional count per muffin 12.5g total fat (7.1g saturated fat); 1087kJ (260 cal); 25.7g carbohydrate; 10g protein; 1.9g fibre

BANANA AND CINNAMON MUFFINS

2 cups (300g) self-raising flour
⅓ cup (50g) plain flour
1 teaspoon ground cinnamon
½ teaspoon bicarbonate of soda
½ cup (110g) firmly packed brown sugar
1 cup mashed banana
2 eggs
¾ cup (180ml) buttermilk
⅓ cup (80ml) vegetable oil
½ teaspoon ground cinnamon, extra
cream cheese topping
125g cream cheese, softened
¼ cup (40g) icing sugar

1 Preheat oven to 200°C/180°C fan-forced. Grease 12-hole (⅓-cup/80ml) muffin pan.
2 Sift flours, cinnamon, soda and sugar into large bowl; stir in banana then combined eggs, buttermilk and oil. Divide mixture among pan holes.
3 Bake muffins about 20 minutes. Stand in pan 5 minutes; turn onto wire rack to cool.
4 Make cream cheese topping.
5 Spread cold muffins with topping; sprinkle with extra cinnamon.
cream cheese topping Beat ingredients in small bowl with electric mixer until smooth.

prep and cook time 40 minutes
makes 12
nutritional count per muffin 10.3g total fat (3.2g saturated fat); 1133kJ (271 cal); 37.9g carbohydrate; 5.8g protein; 1.5g fibre

a *hearty* breakfast

a cuppa on the verandah

Many of life's big questions have been resolved with a mid-morning cuppa and a still-warm biscuit or scone.

ANZAC BISCUITS

1 cup (90g) rolled oats
1 cup (150g) plain flour
1 cup (220g) firmly packed
   brown sugar
½ cup (40g) desiccated coconut
125g butter
2 tablespoons golden syrup
1 tablespoon water
½ teaspoon bicarbonate of soda

1 Preheat oven to 160°C/140°C fan-forced. Grease oven trays; line with baking paper.
2 Combine oats, sifted flour, sugar and coconut in large bowl.
3 Stir butter, syrup and the water in small saucepan over low heat until smooth; stir in soda. Stir into dry ingredients.
4 Roll level tablespoons of mixture into balls; place about 5cm apart on trays, flatten slightly. Bake about 20 minutes; cool on trays.

prep and cook time 35 minutes
makes 25
nutritional count per anzac 5.4g total fat (3.6g saturated fat); 514kJ (123 cal); 17.2g carbohydrate; 1.2g protein; 0.7g fibre

ANZAC BISCUITS EVOLVED DURING WW1, BAKED AS A TREAT TO SEND TO OUR TROOPS ABROAD. THEY'RE MADE FROM A VERY SIMILAR MIX TO THE ARMY RATIONS BUT WITH THE ALL-IMPORTANT, SWEET ADDITIONS OF GOLDEN SYRUP, OATMEAL AND DESICCATED COCONUT.

"Morning tea is a little ritual in our home. It can sweeten the rest of the day."
– Jean Kelly, Dubbo, New South Wales

ABOVE PIKELETS
LEFT VANILLA KISSES

PIKELETS

1 cup (150g) self-raising flour
¼ cup (55g) caster sugar
pinch bicarbonate of soda
1 egg, beaten lightly
¾ cup (180g) milk, approximately

1 Sift dry ingredients into medium bowl. Make well in centre; gradually stir in egg and enough milk to give a smooth, pouring consistency.
2 Drop tablespoons of batter into heated oiled large frying pan; allow room for spreading. When bubbles begin to appear, turn pikelets; cook until lightly browned on other side. Serve warm with butter or cream and jam.

prep and cook time 40 minutes
makes 18
nutritional count per pikelet 3.2g total fat (1.5g saturated fat); 882kJ (211 cal); 38.2g carbohydrate; 6.2g protein; 1.3g fibre

VANILLA KISSES

125g butter, softened
½ cup (110g) caster sugar
1 egg
⅓ cup (50g) plain flour
¼ cup (35g) self-raising flour
⅔ cup (100g) cornflour
¼ cup (30g) custard powder

vienna cream
60g butter, softened
½ teaspoon vanilla extract
¾ cup (120g) icing sugar
2 teaspoons milk

1 Preheat oven to 200°C/180°C fan-forced. Grease oven trays; line with baking paper.
2 Beat butter, sugar and egg in small bowl with electric mixer until light and fluffy. Stir in sifted dry ingredients, in two batches.
3 Spoon mixture into piping bag fitted with 1cm-fluted tube. Pipe 3cm rosettes about 3cm apart on trays.
4 Bake biscuits about 10 minutes; cool on trays.
5 Meanwhile, make vienna cream. Sandwich biscuits with vienna cream.
vienna cream Beat butter and extract in small bowl with electric mixer until as white as possible. Gradually beat in sifted icing sugar and milk, in two batches.

prep and cook time 25 minutes
makes 20
nutritional count per kiss 7.8g total fat (5.1g saturated fat); 648kJ (155 cal); 20g carbohydrate; 0.9g protein; 0.2g fibre

HONEY JUMBLES

60g butter
½ cup (110g) firmly packed brown sugar
¾ cup (270g) golden syrup
1 egg, beaten lightly
2½ cups (375g) plain flour
½ cup (75g) self-raising flour
½ teaspoon bicarbonate of soda
1 teaspoon ground cinnamon
½ teaspoon ground clove
2 teaspoons ground ginger
1 teaspoon mixed spice

icing
1 egg white
1½ cups (240g) icing sugar
2 teaspoons plain flour
1 tablespoon lemon juice, approximately
pink food colouring

1 Preheat oven to 160°C/140°C fan-forced. Grease oven trays.
2 Stir butter, sugar and syrup in medium saucepan over low heat until sugar dissolves. Cool 10 minutes.
3 Transfer mixture to large bowl; stir in egg and sifted dry ingredients, in two batches. Knead dough on floured surface until it loses its stickiness. Cover; refrigerate 30 minutes.
4 Divide dough into eight portions. Roll each portion into a 2cm-thick sausage; cut each sausage into five 6cm lengths. Place about 3cm apart on oven trays; round ends with lightly floured fingers, flatten slightly.
5 Bake about 15 minutes; cool on trays.
6 Meanwhile, make icing. Spread jumbles with pink and white icing.
icing Beat egg white lightly in small bowl; gradually stir in sifted icing sugar and flour, then enough juice to make icing spreadable. Place half the mixture in another small bowl; tint with colouring. Keep icings covered with a damp tea towel while in use.

prep and cook time 25 minutes (plus refrigeration)
makes 40
nutritional count per honey jumble 1.5g total fat (0.9g saturated fat); 456kJ (109 cal); 21.9g carbohydrate; 1.5g protein; 0.4g fibre

"You can come out of the stockyards covered in filth, but there's something civilising about washing your hands, stepping onto the verandah and enjoying a pot of leaf tea out of a cup and saucer."
– Tim Hughes, farmer in Glen Innes, New South Wales

a *cuppa* on the verandah

ABOVE TRADITIONAL SHORTBREAD
LEFT ROCK CAKES

TRADITIONAL SHORTBREAD

250g butter, softened
⅓ cup (75g) caster sugar
1 tablespoon water
2 cups (300g) plain flour
½ cup (100g) rice flour
2 tablespoons white sugar

1 Preheat oven to 160°C/140°C fan-forced. Grease oven trays.
2 Beat butter and caster sugar in medium bowl with electric mixer until light and fluffy; stir in the water and sifted flours, in two batches. Knead on floured surface until smooth.
3 Divide dough in half; shape each, on separate trays, into 20cm rounds. Mark each round into 12 wedges; prick with fork. Pinch edges of rounds with fingers; sprinkle with white sugar.
4 Bake shortbread about 40 minutes; stand on trays 5 minutes. Using sharp knife, cut shortbread into wedges along marked lines. Cool on trays.

prep and cook time 1 hour
makes 24
nutritional count per shortbread 8.8g total fat (5.7g saturated fat); 644kJ (154 cal); 17g carbohydrate; 1.7g protein; 0.6g fibre

ROCK CAKES

2 cups (300g) self-raising flour
¼ teaspoon ground cinnamon
⅓ cup (75g) caster sugar
90g butter, chopped
1 cup (160g) sultanas
1 egg, beaten lightly
½ cup (125ml) milk
1 tablespoon caster sugar, extra

1 Preheat oven to 200°C/180°C fan-forced. Grease oven trays.
2 Sift flour, cinnamon and sugar into medium bowl; rub in butter. Stir in sultanas, egg and milk. Do not over-mix.
3 Drop rounded tablespoons of mixture about 5cm apart onto trays; sprinkle with extra sugar.
4 Bake rock cakes about 15 minutes. Cool on trays.

prep and cook time 30 minutes
makes 18
nutritional count per rock cake 4.9g total fat (3g saturated fat); 640kJ (153 cal); 24g carbohydrate; 2.5g protein; 1g fibre

CHOCOLATE CHIP COOKIES

125g butter, softened
½ teaspoon vanilla extract
⅓ cup (75g) caster sugar
⅓ cup (75g) firmly packed brown sugar
1 egg
1 cup (150g) plain flour
½ teaspoon bicarbonate of soda
150g milk eating chocolate, chopped coarsely
½ cup (50g) walnuts, chopped coarsely

1 Preheat oven to 180°C/160°C fan-forced. Grease oven trays; line with baking paper.
2 Beat butter, extract, sugars and egg in small bowl with electric mixer until smooth; do not overbeat. Transfer mixture to medium bowl; stir in sifted flour and soda then chocolate and nuts.
3 Drop level tablespoons of mixture onto trays 5cm apart. Bake about 15 minutes; cool on trays.

prep and cook time 40 minutes
makes 24
nutritional count per cookie 7.9g total fat (4.7g saturated fat); 564kJ (135 cal); 14.3g carbohydrate; 1.5g protein; 0.7g fibre

NOTE THIS RECIPE CALLS FOR COARSELY CHOPPED WALNUTS. TO CHOP THEM, USE A LARGE, HEAVY KNIFE OR PULSE THEM IN A FOOD PROCESSOR: DON'T OVER-PULSE OR THEY'LL TURN TO PASTE.

a *cuppa* on the verandah

TIP ONCE THE BISCUIT COOKING TIME IS UP, TEST IF THEY'RE DONE BY GENTLY PUSHING A BISCUIT WITH YOUR THUMB. IF THE BISCUIT MOVES OR SLIDES (EVEN IF IT'S STILL SOFT), THEY'RE DONE – THEY'LL FIRM AS THEY COOL.

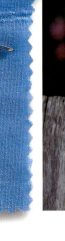

TOP, CENTRE JAM DROPS
ABOVE, LEFT A BOX OF GINGERNUTS MAKES A SWEET GIFT

JAM DROPS

125g butter, softened
½ teaspoon vanilla extract
½ cup (110g) caster sugar
1 cup (120g) almond meal
1 egg
⅔ cup (100g) plain flour
2 tablespoons raspberry jam

1 Preheat oven to 180°C/160°C fan forced. Grease oven trays; line with baking paper.
2 Beat butter, extract, sugar and meal in small bowl with electric mixer until light and fluffy. Add egg, beating until just combined; stir in sifted flour.
3 Drop level tablespoons of mixture on trays 5cm apart. Use handle of wooden spoon to make small hole (about 1cm deep) in top of each biscuit; fill each hole with ¼ teaspoon jam.
4 Bake jam drops about 15 minutes; cool on trays.

prep and cook time 45 minutes
makes 24
nutritional count per jam drop 7.3g total fat (3.1g saturated fat); 464kJ (111 cal); 9.3g carbohydrate; 1.8g protein; 0.6g fibre

GINGERNUTS

90g butter
⅓ cup (75g) firmly packed brown sugar
⅓ cup (115g) golden syrup
1⅓ cups (200g) plain flour
¾ teaspoon bicarbonate of soda
1 tablespoon ground ginger
1 teaspoon ground cinnamon
¼ teaspoon ground clove

1 Preheat oven to 180°C/160°C fan-forced. Grease oven trays.
2 Stir butter, sugar and syrup in medium saucepan over low heat until smooth. Remove from heat; stir in sifted dry ingredients. Cool 10 minutes.
3 Roll rounded teaspoons of mixture into balls. Place about 3cm apart on trays; flatten slightly.
4 Bake gingernuts about 10 minutes; cool on trays.

prep and cook time 25 minutes (plus cooling)
makes 32
nutritional count per gingernut 2.4g total fat (1.5g saturated fat); 263kJ (63 cal); 9.5g carbohydrate; 0.7g protein; 0.3g fibre

a *cuppa* on the verandah

48

the *country* table

"Having a cuppa on the verandah might involve a bit of strategic planning for the farm or talking prices with an agent, or just a chance to communicate with each other. But it always involves a piece of home-made cake or a bickie from the tin."

– Sal Molesworth, Glen Innes, New South Wales

FIG JAM AND RAISIN ROLLS

125g butter
½ cup (100g) firmly packed brown sugar
2 eggs
1½ cups (225g) self-raising flour
½ cup (160g) fig jam
1 cup (170g) chopped raisins
½ cup (125ml) milk

1 Preheat oven to 200°C/180°C fan forced. Grease two 8cm x 19cm nut roll tins; line bases with baking paper. Place tins upright on oven tray.
2 Beat butter and sugar in small bowl with electric mixer until light and fluffy; beat in eggs, one at a time. Transfer to medium bowl; stir in flour, jam, raisins and milk, in two batches. Spoon mixture into tins; replace lids.
3 Bake rolls, tins standing upright, about 50 minutes. Stand rolls 5 minutes, remove lids (top and bottom); shake tins gently to release rolls onto wire rack to cool.

prep and cook time 1 hour 10 minutes
serves 20 (makes 2 rolls)
nutritional count per serving 6.1g total fat (3.7g saturated fat); 686kJ (164 cal); 24.5g carbohydrate; 2.2g protein; 0.9g fibre

JAM ROLL

3 eggs, separated
½ cup (110g) caster sugar
2 tablespoons hot milk
¾ cup (110g) self-raising flour
¼ cup (110g) caster sugar, extra
½ cup (160g) jam, warmed

1 Preheat oven to 200°C/180°C fan forced. Grease 25cm x 30cm swiss roll pan; line base with baking paper, extending paper 5cm over short sides.
2 Beat egg whites in small bowl with electric mixer until soft peaks form; add sugar, 1 tablespoon at a time, beating until dissolved between additions. With motor operating, add egg yolks, one at a time, beating until mixture is pale and thick; this will take about 10 minutes.
3 Pour hot milk down side of bowl; add triple-sifted flour. Working quickly, use plastic spatula to fold milk and flour through egg mixture. Pour mixture into pan, gently spreading evenly into corners.
4 Bake cake about 8 minutes.
5 Meanwhile, place a piece of baking paper cut the same size as pan on board or bench; sprinkle evenly with extra sugar.
6 Turn cake onto sugared paper; peel away lining paper. Use serrated knife to trim crisp edges from all sides of cake.
7 Using paper as a guide, gently roll cake loosely from one of the short sides. Unroll; spread evenly with jam. Reroll cake from same short side. Cool.

prep and cook time 30 minutes
serves 10
nutritional count per serving 1.9g total fat (0.6g saturated fat); 819kJ (196 cal); 40.5g carbohydrate; 3.3g protein; 0.6g fibre

TIP THERE ARE SEVERAL DIFFERENT SIZES AND TYPES OF NUT ROLL TINS AVAILABLE, AND IT IS IMPORTANT THAT YOU DO NOT FILL THEM WITH TOO MUCH MIXTURE. AS A LOOSE GUIDE, THE TINS SHOULD BE FILLED JUST A LITTLE OVER HALFWAY. WELL-CLEANED FRUIT JUICE CANS MAY BE USED INSTEAD OF THE NUT ROLL TINS; USE A DOUBLE THICKNESS OF FOIL AS A SUBSTITUTE FOR THE LIDS.

RIGHT FIG JAM AND RAISIN ROLLS
BELOW JAM ROLL

51

a *cuppa* on the verandah

DATE AND WALNUT ROLLS

60g butter

1 cup (250ml) boiling water

1 cup (180g) finely chopped dried dates

½ teaspoon bicarbonate of soda

1 cup (200g) firmly packed brown sugar

2 cups (300g) self-raising flour

½ cup (65g) coarsely chopped walnuts

1 egg, beaten lightly

1 Preheat oven to 200°C/180°C fan forced. Grease two 8cm x 19cm nut roll tins; line bases with baking paper. Place tins upright on oven tray.
2 Using wooden spoon, stir butter and the water in medium saucepan over low heat until butter melts. Transfer mixture to large bowl; stir in dates and soda, then sugar, flour, nuts and egg. Spoon mixture into tins; replace lids.
3 Bake rolls, tins standing upright, about 50 minutes. Stand rolls 5 minutes, remove lids (top and bottom); shake tins gently to release rolls onto wire rack to cool.

prep and cook time 1 hour 10 minutes
makes 20
nutritional count per roll 5g total fat (1.9g saturated fat); 702kJ (168 cal); 27.4g carbohydrate; 2.5g protein; 1.6g fibre

MONTE CARLO BISCUITS

180g butter, softened
1 teaspoon vanilla extract
½ cup (110g) firmly packed brown sugar
1 egg
1¼ cups (185g) self-raising flour
¾ cup (105g) plain flour
¼ teaspoon bicarbonate of soda
⅔ cup (50g) desiccated coconut
⅓ cup (110g) raspberry jam

vienna cream
60g butter
½ teaspoon vanilla extract
¾ cup (120g) icing sugar
2 teaspoons milk

1 Preheat oven to 200°C/180°C fan-forced. Grease oven trays; line with baking paper.
2 Beat butter, extract and sugar in small bowl with electric mixer until just combined; beat in egg. Stir in sifted flours, soda and coconut in two batches.
3 Roll 2 level teaspoons of mixture into ovals; place on trays about 5cm apart. Flatten slightly; use back of fork to roughen surface. Bake about 7 minutes.
4 Meanwhile, make vienna cream.
5 Lift biscuits onto wire rack to cool. Sandwich biscuits with vienna cream and jam.
vienna cream Beat butter, extract and sifted icing sugar in small bowl with electric mixer until fluffy; beat in milk.

prep and cook time 40 minutes
makes 28
nutritional count per monte carlo 8.5g total fat (5.7g saturated fat); 656kJ (157 cal); 18.3g carbohydrate; 1.5g protein; 0.7g fibre

"My morning coffee is my solace, my non-negotiable time, my thinking time. I look out across the paddocks and dream about my next project on the farm."

– Virginia Imhoff, Kingston, Victoria

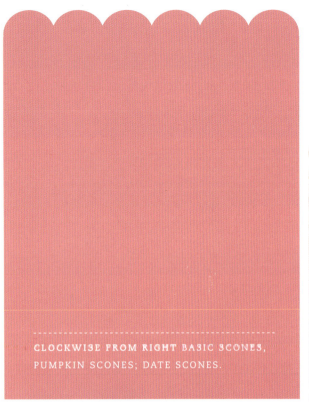

CLOCKWISE FROM RIGHT BASIC SCONES, PUMPKIN SCONES; DATE SCONES.

BASIC SCONES

2½ cups (375g) self-raising flour

1 tablespoon caster sugar

¼ teaspoon salt

30g butter

¾ cup (180ml) milk

½ cup (125ml) water, approximately

1 Preheat oven to 220°C/200°C fan forced. Grease deep 19cm-square cake pan.
2 Sift flour, sugar and salt into large bowl; rub in butter with fingertips.
3 Make well in centre of flour mixture; add milk and almost all of the water. Using a knife, "cut" the milk and the water through the flour mixture to mix to a soft, sticky dough. Add remaining water only if needed. Knead dough on floured surface until smooth.
4 Use hand to press dough out evenly to 2cm thickness. Cut as many 4.5cm rounds as you can from dough. Place rounds side by side, just touching, in pan. Gently knead scraps of dough together; repeat pressing and cutting of dough, place in same pan. Brush tops with a little extra milk.
5 Bake scones about 15 minutes or until browned and scones sound hollow when tapped firmly on the top with fingers.

prep and cook time 45 minutes
makes 16
nutritional count per scone 2.3g total fat (1.3g saturated fat); 443kJ (106 cal); 18.2g carbohydrate; 2.7g protein; 0.9g fibre

variation

date scones When making the basic scone mixture, stir ¾ cup (120g) finely chopped seeded dried dates into the flour mixture after the butter has been rubbed in. Also, replace the milk and water with 1¼ cups (310ml) buttermilk.

prep and cook time 45 minutes
makes 16
nutritional count per scone 2.4g total fat (1.3g saturated fat); 552kJ (132 cal); 21.7g carbohydrate; 3.8g protein; 3.4g fibre

PUMPKIN SCONES

40g butter

¼ cup (55g) caster sugar

1 egg, beaten lightly

¾ cup cooked mashed pumpkin

2½ cups (375g) self-raising flour

½ teaspoon ground nutmeg

⅓ cup (180ml) milk, approximately

1 Preheat oven to 220°C/200°C fan forced. Grease two 20cm-round sandwich pans.
2 Beat butter and sugar in small bowl with electric mixer until light and fluffy; beat in egg.
3 Transfer mixture to large bowl. Stir in pumpkin, then sifted dry ingredients and enough milk to make a soft sticky dough. Knead dough on floured surface until smooth.
4 Use hand to press dough out evenly to 2cm thickness. Cut as many 5cm rounds as you can from dough. Place rounds side by side, just touching, in pans. Gently knead scraps of dough together; repeat pressing and cutting of dough, place in same pan. Brush tops with a little extra milk.
5 Bake scones about 15 minutes or until browned and scones sound hollow when tapped firmly on the top with fingers.

prep and cook time 35 minutes
makes 16
nutritional count per scone 2.9g total fat (1.7g saturated fat); 527kJ (126 cal); 21.1g carbohydrate; 3.2g protein; 1.1g fibre

a *cuppa* on the verandah

let's eat outdoors

It's summertime and the living is easy – filled with picnics, barbecues and sweet, seasonal produce.

GRILLED PORK SAUSAGES WITH FRUIT RELISH

1 tablespoon olive oil
1 small red onion (100g), chopped finely
1 clove garlic, crushed
2 medium pears (460g), chopped finely
¼ cup (55g) finely chopped dried apricots
¼ cup (40g) sultanas, chopped finely
2 tablespoons cider vinegar
2 tablespoons brown sugar
½ teaspoon ground allspice
12 thick pork sausages (1.5kg)

1 Heat oil in medium saucepan; cook onion and garlic, stirring, until onions soften. Add fruit, vinegar, sugar and spice; cook, uncovered, stirring occasionally, about 10 minutes or until mixture is thick and pulpy.
2 Meanwhile, cook sausages on heated oiled grill plate (or grill or barbecue) until cooked through.
3 Serve sausages with fruit relish.

prep and cook time 30 minutes
serves 6
nutritional count per serving 58.7g total fat (22.9g saturated fat); 3252kJ (778 cal); 29.9g carbohydrate; 31g protein; 6.2g fibre

THIS FLAVOUR-PACKED FRUIT RELISH ADDS A SOPHISTICATED TOUCH TO EVERYONE'S TRADITIONAL, FAVOURITE COMFORT MEAL: BANGERS AND MASH.

"Simple, generous, hearty food served in a relaxed mode – that is the essence of country cooking".
– Stefano di Pieri

ABOVE CHICKEN LIVER PATE WITH PORT
LEFT QUICHE LORRAINE

CHICKEN LIVER PATE WITH PORT

500g chicken livers

⅓ cup (80ml) port

120g butter

1 medium white onion (150g), chopped finely

1 clove garlic, crushed

½ teaspoon dried tarragon

2 tablespoons brandy

1 tablespoon tomato paste

⅓ cup (80g) sour cream

1 Trim and wash livers; cut in half. Combine livers in small bowl with port; cover. Stand 2 hours; strain.
2 Melt a quarter of the butter in medium frying pan; cook onion and garlic, stirring constantly over medium heat about 3 minutes or until onion is soft. Add livers to pan; stir constantly about 5 minutes or until livers are just changed in colour. Stir in tarragon and brandy; bring to the boil. Reduce heat; simmer, uncovered, about 3 minutes or until livers are tender.
3 Melt a quarter of the butter in saucepan. Blend or process liver mixture until smooth. Add tomato paste and sour cream; blend until combined. While motor is operating, gradually add melted butter.
4 Pour pâté into four ½-cup (125ml) serving dishes; garnish with sprig of herbs or bay leaf, if desired. Cover; refrigerate 2 hours.
5 Coarsely chop remaining butter; melt in small saucepan over low heat, without stirring. Stand a few minutes, then use spoon to carefully remove and discard whitish-coloured scum floating on surface. Carefully pour remaining clear liquid into jug, leaving whitish milky deposits in the pan; discard deposits.
6 Gently pour a thin layer of clarified butter over pâté; refrigerate overnight.

prep and cook time 40 minutes
(plus standing and refrigeration)
serves 10
nutritional count per serving 15g total fat (9.2g saturated fat); 836kJ (200 cal); 3g carbohydrate; 9.7g protein; 0.3g fibre

QUICHE LORRAINE

1¾ cups (255g) plain flour

150g cold butter, chopped

1 egg yolk

2 teaspoons lemon juice, approximately

⅓ cup (80ml) cold water

1 medium brown onion (150g), chopped finely

3 bacon rashers (210g), chopped finely

3 eggs

300ml cream

½ cup (125ml) milk

¾ cup (120g) grated cheddar cheese

1 Sift flour into bowl; rub in butter. Add egg yolk, juice and enough water to make ingredients cling together. Knead gently on floured surface until smooth. Cover; refrigerate 30 minutes.
2 Preheat oven to 200°C/180°C fan-forced.
3 Roll pastry between sheets of baking paper large enough to line a deep 23cm loose-base flan tin. Lift pastry into flan tin; gently ease pastry into side of tin. Trim edge. Place flan on oven tray.
4 Line pastry with baking paper, fill with dried beans or rice. Bake for 10 minutes; remove paper and beans carefully. Bake pastry about 10 minutes or until golden brown; cool to room temperature.
5 Reduce oven to 180°C/160°C fan-forced.
6 Cook onion and bacon in oiled small frying pan until onion is soft; drain away excess fat. Cool; sprinkle into pastry case.
7 Whisk eggs in medium bowl; whisk in cream, milk and cheese until just combined. Pour into pastry case.
8 Bake quiche about 35 minutes or until filling is set and brown. Stand 5 minutes before removing from tin.

prep and cook time 1 hour 30 minutes
(plus refrigeration and standing)
serves 6
nutritional count per serving 58.1g total fat (35.4g saturated fat); 3127kJ (748 cal); 34.8g carbohydrate; 22g protein; 1.9g fibre

let's eat *outdoors*

"Lingering meals outdoors are so refreshing. You can drink up the landscape and there is always a cattle dog or two standing sentinel to catch the crumbs."
– Claire MacTaggart, Rockhampton, Queensland

COUNTRY STYLE TERRINE

350g chicken thigh fillets, chopped coarsely

400g boned pork belly, rind removed, chopped coarsely

300g piece calves liver, trimmed, chopped coarsely

3 bacon rashers (210g), rind removed, chopped coarsely

3 cloves garlic, crushed

2 teaspoons finely chopped fresh thyme

10 juniper berries, crushed

2 tablespoons port

¼ cup (60ml) dry white wine

1 egg

¼ cup (35g) roasted, shelled pistachios

1 Preheat oven to 150°C/130°C fan-forced. Oil 1.5-litre (6-cup) ovenproof terrine dish.
2 Blend or process meats, separately, until coarsely minced; combine in large bowl with remaining ingredients.
3 Press meat mixture into terrine dish; cover with foil. Place terrine dish in baking dish; pour enough boiling water into baking dish to come halfway up side of terrine dish. Bake 1 hour. Uncover; bake a further 1 hour or until cooked through.
4 Remove terrine dish from baking dish; cover terrine with baking paper. Weight with another dish filled with heavy cans; cool 10 minutes then refrigerate overnight.
5 Turn terrine onto serving plate; serve sliced, at room temperature, with french bread and cornichons, if desired.

prep and cook time 2 hours 20 minutes (plus refrigeration)
serves 6
nutritional count per serving 30.1g total fat (9.6g saturated fat); 2019kJ (483 cal); 3.6g carbohydrate; 46.2g protein; 0.8g fibre

ABOVE GOOD, OLD-FASHIONED CHICKEN SALAD
LEFT RISSOLES WITH GRILLED ONIONS

GOOD, OLD-FASHIONED CHICKEN SALAD

1 litre (4 cups) boiling water

1 litre (4 cups) chicken stock

700g chicken breast fillets

1 long french bread stick, sliced thinly

2 tablespoons olive oil

½ cup (150g) mayonnaise

½ cup (120g) sour cream

2 tablespoons lemon juice

4 trimmed celery stalks (400g), sliced thinly

1 medium white onion (150g), chopped finely

3 large dill pickles (150g), sliced thinly

2 tablespoons finely chopped fresh flat-leaf parsley

1 tablespoon finely chopped fresh tarragon

1 large butter lettuce, leaves separated

1 Bring the water and stock to the boil in large frying pan; poach chicken, covered, about 10 minutes or until cooked through. Cool chicken in liquid 10 minutes; slice thinly. Discard liquid.
2 Meanwhile, brush both sides of bread slices with oil; toast under preheated grill until browned lightly both sides.
3 Whisk mayonnaise, cream and juice in small bowl.
4 Place chicken in large bowl with celery, onion, pickle and herbs; toss gently to combine.
5 Place lettuce leaves on serving platter; top with salad and bread, drizzle with mayonnaise mixture.

prep and cook time 50 minutes *serves* 4
nutritional count per serving 41g total fat (12.5g saturated fat); 3323kJ (795 cal); 52g carbohydrate; 51.7g protein; 6.4g fibre

RISSOLES WITH GRILLED ONIONS

2 rindless bacon rashers (135g), chopped finely

1 small brown onion (80g), chopped finely

500g beef mince

1 cup (70g) stale breadcrumbs

1 egg

2 tablespoons barbecue sauce

1 tablespoon worcestershire sauce

1 tablespoon olive oil

3 medium brown onions (450g), sliced thinly

2 tablespoons brown sugar

1 tablespoon malt vinegar

1 Cook bacon and onion in oiled medium frying pan, stirring, until onion softens. Cool.
2 Combine mince, breadcrumbs, egg, sauces and bacon mixture in large bowl; shape mixture into 12 rissoles.
3 Cook rissoles on heated barbecue grill plate until cooked as desired
4 Meanwhile, heat oil on barbecue flat plate; cook onions, stirring, until browned lightly. Add sugar and vinegar; cook, stirring, about 5 minutes or until onions caramelise.
5 Serve rissoles with grilled onions and, if desired, a green salad.

prep and cook time 40 minutes *serves* 4
nutritional count per serving 19.9g total fat (6.5g saturated fat); 1944kJ (465 cal); 31.7g carbohydrate; 38.3g protein; 3.7g fibre

let's eat *outdoors*

"There's a growing disconnect between people and the source of the food that sustains them. Out here, there's no middle man between the paddock and the plate."
– Tim Hughes, farmer in Glen Innes, New South Wales

BARBECUED LAMB CHOPS WITH MUSTARD AND THYME MARINADE

2 tablespoons olive oil

2 cloves garlic, crushed

2 tablespoons wholegrain mustard

2 tablespoons lemon juice

2 teaspoons finely chopped fresh thyme

4 forequarter lamb chops (760g)

1 Combine oil, garlic, mustard, juice and thyme in large bowl; add chops, turn to coat in marinade. Cover; refrigerate 3 hours or overnight.
2 Cook drained chops on heated oiled grill plate (or grill or barbecue) until browned both sides and cooked as desired.
3 Serve chops, if desired, with vegetables and extra mustard.

prep and cook time 30 minutes (plus refrigeration)
serves 4
nutritional count per serving 17.5g total fat (5.1g saturated fat); 1158kJ (277 cal); 0.8g carbohydrate; 29g protein; 0.5g fibre

SAVOURY-GLAZED MEATLOAF

750g beef mince

1 cup (70g) stale breadcrumbs

1 medium brown onion (150g), chopped finely

1 egg

2 tablespoons tomato sauce

1 tablespoon worcestershire sauce

185g can evaporated milk

2 teaspoons mustard powder

1 tablespoon brown sugar

½ teaspoon mustard powder, extra

¼ cup (60ml) tomato sauce, extra

1 Preheat oven to 180°C/160°C fan-forced. Oil 14cm x 21cm loaf pan.
2 Combine beef, breadcrumbs, onion, egg, sauces, milk and mustard in medium bowl. Press mixture into pan. Turn pan upside-down onto a foil-lined oven tray. Leave pan in place. Cook 15 minutes.
3 Meanwhile, combine sugar, extra mustard and extra tomato sauce in small bowl.
4 Remove loaf from oven; remove pan. Brush loaf well with glaze, return loaf to oven; cook 45 minutes or until well browned and cooked through.
5 Serve meatloaf, if desired, with rocket leaves and tomato wedges.

prep and cook time 1 hour
serves 4
nutritional count per serving 19.9g total fat (10g saturated fat); 1986kJ (475 cal); 29.1g carbohydrate; 45.8g protein; 1.8g fibre

> "A handful of salad leaves, eggs from the chookhouse and homegrown lamb. It's so sweet to enjoy the fruits of your labour."
> – Sal Molesworth,
> Glen Innes, New South Wales

RIGHT BARBECUED LAMB CHOPS WITH MUSTARD AND THYME MARINADE
BELOW SAVOURY-GLAZED MEATLOAF

let's eat *outdoors*

TIPS SMOKING CHIPS AND SMOKE BOXES ARE AVAILABLE FROM BARBECUE SPECIALTY SHOPS. WHEN USING INDIRECT HEAT WITH A GAS BURNER, PLACE THE FOOD IN A PREHEATED, COVERED BARBECUE, THEN TURN THE BURNERS DIRECTLY UNDER THE FOOD OFF, WHILE KEEPING THE SIDE BURNERS ON. WITH A CHARCOAL BARBECUE, METAL BARS HOLD TWO LAYERS OF COALS AGAINST THE SIDES OF THE BARBECUE, LEAVING THE CENTRE OF THE BARBECUE RACK EMPTY. A DISPOSABLE ALUMINIUM BAKING DISH CAN BE PLACED HERE TO CATCH FAT DRIPS, IF DESIRED.

GARLIC AND ROSEMARY SMOKED LAMB

1kg boned, rolled lamb loin
4 cloves garlic, halved
8 fresh rosemary sprigs
1 teaspoon dried chilli flakes
1 tablespoon olive oil
250g smoking chips

1 Pierce lamb in eight places with sharp knife; push garlic and rosemary into cuts. Sprinkle lamb with chilli; rub with oil. Cover; refrigerate 3 hours or overnight.
2 Soak smoking chips in large bowl of water 2 hours.
3 Cook lamb, uncovered, on heated oiled barbecue until browned all over. Place drained smoking chips in smoke box on barbecue next to lamb. Cook lamb in covered barbecue, using indirect heat and following manufacturer's instructions, about 40 minutes or until cooked as desired.

prep and cook time 1 hour
(plus refrigeration and soaking)
serves 6
nutritional count per serving 17.8g total fat (7.1g saturated fat); 1250kJ (299 cal); 0.2g carbohydrate; 35g protein; 0.3g fibre

the *country* table

"Traditionally, country cooks had to be creative, using what was to hand in new and appetising ways. The recipes are always simple, relying on fresh ingredients and straightforward cooking techniques. That is why we go on loving them."
— Pamela Clark

CORNED BEEF WITH PARSLEY SAUCE

1.5kg whole piece beef corned silverside
2 bay leaves
6 black peppercorns
1 large brown onion (200g), quartered
1 large carrot (180g), chopped coarsely
1 tablespoon brown malt vinegar
¼ cup (50g) firmly packed brown sugar

parsley sauce
30g butter
¼ cup (35g) plain flour
2½ cups (625ml) milk
⅓ cup (40g) grated cheddar cheese
⅓ cup finely chopped fresh flat-leaf parsley
1 tablespoon mild mustard

1 Place beef, bay leaves, peppercorns, onion, carrot, vinegar and half of the sugar in large saucepan. Add enough water to just cover beef; simmer, covered, about 2 hours or until beef is tender. Cool beef 1 hour in liquid in pan.
2 Remove beef from pan; discard liquid. Sprinkle sheet of foil with remaining sugar, wrap beef in foil; stand 20 minutes before serving.
3 Make parsley sauce.
4 Serve sliced corned beef with parsley sauce.
parsley sauce Melt butter in small saucepan, add flour; cook, stirring, until bubbling. Gradually stir in milk; cook, stirring, until sauce boils and thickens. Remove from heat; stir in cheese, parsley and mustard.

prep and cook time 2 hours 30 minutes (plus standing and cooling)
serves 4
nutritional count per serving 35.8g total fat (19.3g saturated fat); 3520kJ (842 cal); 31g carbohydrate; 97g protein; 2.5g fibre

let's eat *outdoors*

DAMPER

3 cups (450g) self-raising flour

30g butter

½ cup (125ml) milk

1 cup (250ml) water, approximately

1 Preheat oven to 180°C/160°C fan-forced. Grease oven tray.
2 Sift flour into bowl; rub in butter. Make well in centre, add milk and enough water to mix to a soft sticky dough. Knead on floured surface until smooth.
3 Press dough into 15cm circle, place on tray. Cut a cross through dough, about 1cm deep. Brush top with a little extra milk or water; dust with a little extra flour.
4 Bake 30 minutes or until damper sounds hollow when tapped.

prep and cook time 45 minutes *serves* 6
nutritional count per serving 5.8g total fat (3.4g saturated fat); 1292kJ (309 cal); 53.9g carbohydrate; 8.1g protein; 2.9g fibre

OAK LEAF AND HERB SALAD WITH DIJON VINAIGRETTE

1 green oak leaf lettuce, leaves separated

¼ cup coarsely chopped fresh chives

½ cup firmly packed fresh flat-leaf parsley leaves

½ cup firmly packed fresh chervil leaves

dijon vinaigrette

2 tablespoons olive oil

2 tablespoons white wine vinegar

1 tablespoon dijon mustard

2 teaspoons white sugar

1 Place ingredients for dijon vinaigrette in screw-top jar; shake well. Add vinaigrette to medium bowl with salad ingredients; toss gently to combine.

prep time 10 minutes *serves* 6
nutritional count per serving 6.2g total fat (0.9g saturated fat); 288kJ (69 cal); 2g carbohydrate; 0.7g protein; 1.1g fibre

POTATO SALAD

2kg potatoes, peeled

2 tablespoons cider vinegar

8 green onions, sliced thinly

¼ cup finely chopped fresh flat-leaf parsley

mayonnaise

2 egg yolks

1 teaspoon dijon mustard

2 teaspoons lemon juice

1 cup (250ml) vegetable oil

2 tablespoons hot water, approximately

1 Cut potatoes into 1.5cm pieces. Place potato in large saucepan, barely cover with cold water; cover saucepan, bring to the boil. Reduce heat; simmer, uncovered, stirring occasionally, until just tender. Drain, spread potato on a tray; sprinkle with vinegar. Cool 10 minutes. Cover; refrigerate until cold.
2 Meanwhile, make mayonnaise.
3 Place potato in large bowl with mayonnaise, onion and parsley; mix gently to combine.
mayonnaise Blend or process egg yolks, mustard and juice until smooth. With motor operating, gradually add oil in a thin, steady stream; process until mixture thickens. Add as much of the hot water as needed to thin mayonnaise.

prep and cook time 40 minutes (plus refrigeration)
serves 8
nutritional count per serving 30.4g total fat (4.1g saturated fat); 1739kJ (416 cal); 28.4g carbohydrate; 6.1g protein; 3.7g fibre

TIP WHETHER YOU LIVE ON A COUNTRY PROPERTY OR IN A CITY APARTMENT YOU CAN ALWAYS GROW YOUR OWN HERBS. PARSLEY, MINT, BASIL AND CHIVES ARE EASY TO GROW IN POTS AND ARE ALWAYS HANDY IN COOKING.

TOP, CENTRE DAMPER
ABOVE, LEFT OAK LEAF AND HERB SALAD
ABOVE POTATO SALAD

let's eat *outdoors*

"I love recreating classic recipes inspired by the time-honoured tradition of country cooks. They are always so honest."
— Pamela Clark

ABOVE BERRY FRANGIPANE TART
LEFT PASSIONFRUIT FLUMMERY

BERRY FRANGIPANE TART

1 sheet ready-rolled sweet puff pastry

300g frozen mixed berries

frangipane

80g butter, softened

½ teaspoon vanilla extract

⅓ cup (75g) caster sugar

2 egg yolks

1 tablespoon plain flour

1 cup (120g) almond meal

1 Preheat oven to 220°C/200°C fan-forced. Grease 20cm x 30cm lamington pan.
2 Roll pastry until large enough to cover base and sides of pan; line pan with pastry, press into sides. Prick pastry all over with fork; freeze 5 minutes.
3 Place another lamington pan on top of pastry; bake 5 minutes. Remove top pan; bake further 5 minutes or until pastry is browned lightly. Cool 5 minutes.
4 Reduce oven to 180°C/160°C fan-forced.
5 Meanwhile, make frangipane.
6 Spread frangipane over pastry base. Sprinkle with berries, press into frangipane. Bake about 30 minutes or until browned lightly.
frangipane Beat butter, extract, sugar and egg yolks in small bowl with electric mixer until light and fluffy. Stir in flour and meal.

prep and cook time 50 minutes
serves 6
nutritional count per serving 30.2g total fat (11.9g saturated fat); 1722kJ (412 cal); 26.4g carbohydrate; 7.7g protein; 3.3g fibre

PASSIONFRUIT FLUMMERY

1 tablespoon gelatine

½ cup (110g) caster sugar

2 tablespoons plain flour

¾ cup (180g) water

1 cup (250ml) orange juice, strained

⅔ cup (160ml) passionfruit pulp

1 Combine gelatine, sugar and flour in pan, gradually stir in water. Stir over heat until mixture boils and thickens. Transfer to medium bowl; stir in juice and passionfruit pulp. Refrigerate until mixture starts to set around edge of bowl.
2 Beat mixture with electric mixer about 10 minutes or until thick and creamy. Pour into six ¾-cup (180ml) serving glasses. Cover; refrigerate 3 hours or overnight.
3 Serve flummery with cream and extra passionfruit pulp, if desired.

prep and cook time 20 minutes (plus refrigeration)
serves 6
nutritional count per serving 0.2g total fat (0g saturated fat); 502kJ (120 cal); 24.4g carbohydrate; 3g protein; 3.9g fibre

LEMON MERINGUE PIE

½ cup (75g) cornflour
1 cup (220g) caster sugar
½ cup (125ml) lemon juice
1¼ cups (310ml) water
2 teaspoons finely grated lemon rind
60g unsalted butter, chopped
3 eggs, separated
½ cup (110g) caster sugar, extra

pastry
1½ cups (225g) plain flour
1 tablespoon icing sugar
140g cold butter, chopped
1 egg yolk
2 tablespoons cold water

1 Make pastry.
2 Grease 24cm-round loose-based fluted flan tin. Roll pastry between sheets of baking paper until large enough to line tin. Ease pastry into tin, press into base and side; trim edge. Cover; refrigerate 30 minutes.
3 Preheat oven to 240°C/220°C fan-forced.
4 Place tin on oven tray. Line pastry case with baking paper; fill with dried beans or rice. Bake 15 minutes; remove paper and beans. Bake about 10 minutes; cool pie shell, turn oven off.
5 Meanwhile, combine cornflour and sugar in medium saucepan; gradually stir in juice and the water until smooth. Cook, stirring, over high heat, until mixture boils and thickens. Reduce heat; simmer, stirring, 1 minute. Remove from heat; stir in rind, butter and egg yolks. Cool 10 minutes.
6 Spread lemon filling into pie shell. Cover; refrigerate 2 hours.
7 Preheat oven to 240°C/220°C fan-forced.
8 Beat egg whites in small bowl with electric mixer until soft peaks form; gradually add extra sugar, beating until sugar dissolves.
9 Roughen surface of filling with fork before spreading with meringue mixture. Bake about 2 minutes or until browned lightly.

pastry Process flour, icing sugar and butter until crumbly. Add egg yolk and the water; process until ingredients come together. Knead dough on floured surface until smooth. Cover; refrigerate 30 minutes.

prep and cook time 1 hour (plus refrigeration)
serves 10
nutritional count per serving 18.9g total fat (11.6g saturated fat); 1772kJ (424 cal); 57.7g carbohydrate; 5g protein; 0.9g fibre

THE TARTNESS OF THIS PIE DEPENDS ON THE LEMONS YOU USE AND THE FLAVOUR WILL VARY SLIGHTLY EVERY TIME YOU MAKE THE FILLING. WHEN SIMMERING THE BOILED AND THICKENED FILLING, YOU MUST STIR CONTINUALLY: IT'S THICK AND WILL BURN IF YOU'RE NOT CAREFUL.

CLASSIC TRIFLE

85g packet raspberry jelly crystals

250g sponge cake, cut into 3cm pieces

¼ cup (60ml) sweet sherry

¼ cup (30g) custard powder

¼ cup (55g) caster sugar

½ teaspoon vanilla extract

1½ cups (375ml) milk

825g can sliced peaches, drained

300ml thickened cream

2 tablespoons flaked almonds, roasted

1 Make jelly according to directions on packet; pour into shallow container. Refrigerate 20 minutes or until jelly is almost set.
2 Arrange cake in 3-litre (12-cup) bowl; sprinkle with sherry.
3 Blend custard powder, sugar and extract with a little of the milk in small saucepan; stir in remaining milk. Stir over heat until mixture boils and thickens. Cover surface with plastic wrap; cool.
4 Pour jelly over cake; refrigerate 15 minutes. Top with peaches. Stir one-third of the cream into custard; pour over peaches.
5 Whip remaining cream; spread over custard, sprinkle with nuts. Refrigerate 3 hours or overnight.

prep and cook time 40 minutes (plus refrigeration)
serves 8
nutritional count per serving 19.7g total fat (10.9g saturated fat); 1689kJ (404 cal); 47g carbohydrate; 7.1g protein; 1.6g fibre

PAVLOVA

4 egg whites

1 cup (220g) caster sugar

½ teaspoon vanilla extract

¾ teaspoon white vinegar

300ml thickened cream, whipped

250g strawberries, halved

1 Preheat oven to 120°C/100°C fan-forced. Line oven tray with foil; grease foil, dust with cornflour, shake away excess. Mark 18cm-circle on foil.
2 Beat egg whites in small bowl with electric mixer until soft peaks form; gradually add sugar, beating until sugar dissolves. Add extract and vinegar; beat until combined.
3 Spread meringue into circle on foil, building up at the side to 8cm in height.
4 Smooth side and top of pavlova gently. Using spatula blade, mark decorative grooves around side of pavlova; smooth top again.
5 Bake about 1½ hours. Turn off oven; cool pavlova in oven with door ajar. When pavlova is cold, cut around top edge (the crisp meringue top will fall slightly on top of the marshmallow). Serve pavlova topped with whipped cream and strawberries; dust lightly with sifted icing sugar, if desired.

prep and cook time 2 hours (plus cooling)
serves 8
nutritional count per serving 14g total fat (9.2g saturated fat); 1078kJ (258 cal); 29.6g carbohydrate; 3.1g protein; 0.7g fibre

The pavlova is named after Anna Pavlova, a ballerina who toured Australia and New Zealand in the 1920s. Its invention is still claimed and disputed by both countries.

RIGHT CLASSIC TRIFLE
BELOW PAVLOVA

ABOVE IMPOSSIBLE PIE
LEFT SUPERB SOUR CREAM CHEESECAKE

IMPOSSIBLE PIE

½ cup (75g) plain flour

1 cup (220g) caster sugar

¾ cup (60g) desiccated coconut

4 eggs

1 teaspoon vanilla extract

125g butter, melted

½ cup (40g) flaked almonds

2 cups (500ml) milk

1 Preheat oven to 180°C/160°C fan-forced. Grease deep 24cm pie dish.
2 Combine sifted flour, sugar, coconut, eggs, extract, butter and half the nuts in large bowl; gradually add milk, stirring, until combined. Pour mixture into dish.
3 Bake pie 35 minutes. Remove pie from oven, sprinkle remaining nuts over pie; bake 10 minutes. Serve pie with cream or fruit, if desired.

prep and cook time 55 minutes
serves 8
nutritional count per serving 25.7g total fat (15.4g saturated fat); 1747kJ (418 cal); 38.2g carbohydrate; 8.1g protein; 1.9g fibre

SUPERB SOUR CREAM CHEESECAKE

250g packet plain sweet biscuits

150g butter, melted

250g packet cream cheese, softened

250g cottage cheese

3 eggs

1 cup (220g) caster sugar

2 tablespoons cornflour

½ cup (125ml) milk

1 cup (240g) sour cream

1 tablespoon finely grated lemon rind

1 teaspoon lemon juice

1 Preheat oven to 180°C/160°C fan-forced.
2 Blend or process biscuits until mixture resembles fine breadcrumbs. Add butter; process until combined. Press biscuit mixture evenly over base and side of 20cm springform tin, place on oven tray; refrigerate about 30 minutes or until firm.
3 Meanwhile, beat cheeses together until smooth. Beat in eggs, one at a time. Stir in sugar and cornflour then milk, cream, rind and juice. Pour into crumb crust.
4 Bake cheesecake about 50 minutes. Cool in oven with door ajar. Refrigerate overnight.

prep and cook time 1 hour 20 minutes (plus refrigeration)
serves 8
nutritional count per serving 45.3g total fat (28.1g saturated fat); 2704kJ (54.5 cal); 54.5g carbohydrate; 8.5g protein; 0.7g fibre

let's eat outdoors

feeding the shearers

COOKING FOR A VISITING TEAM OF SHEARERS IS A HIGHLY-TUNED SKILL REQUIRING PRECISION TIMING, GENEROUS SERVINGS AND ENERGY-PACKED MEALS.

The work of shearers has been paid tribute in the poetry of Henry Lawson, the paintings of Tom Roberts and in endless eulogies on the bush. But behind the romantic imagery of muscle-bound legends and loveable larrikins was a lot of backbreaking hard work and sweat. And not just for the shearers.

While the shearers were in the steaming shearing sheds bent over their quivering subjects, the farm kitchens would be steaming and bubbling away with pots full of hearty fare being prepared with military precision by the farmers' wives and shearers' cooks. And not much has changed today.

Shear hard work Catering for a team of shearers is an unsung logistical feat. It involves cooking enough food for a team of hungry men at least three times a day – for morning tea (commonly called 'smoko'), lunch and afternoon tea. And on the big, remote outback stations, where the shearing teams often stay for the duration of the shearing season, it means providing breakfasts and dinners too.

Against the clock The shearing day is long and runs to a stringent timetable which means the meals must be prepared strictly on time. The focus is on providing hearty and generous – not rich – fare. It has to be sustaining and energy-giving, and carbohydrates and proteins are essential.

Feeding the shearers used to be largely the domain of the farmers' wives, and this tradition still continues in certain farming districts. But on big stations, the shearers are usually part of a contracted team that comes with its own cook and shed hands.

The farmer's wife Jodi Hannemann, a former city girl now married to a sheep farmer on the Eyre Peninsula, in South Australia, is a farmer's wife who still feeds the

86

the *country* table

visiting shearers. When she first moved to the farm as a young bride, it was the one aspect of her new life she found daunting – "almost enough to stop me becoming a farmer's wife."

"The hardest part is running to a time schedule. When you're feeding babies and caring for children, it's not easy to have food ready by a set time."

The shearers' cook Jenny Williams is a shearers' cook from Moree, New South Wales, who spends six months each year working in the remote 'station country' of western Queensland.

Jenny cooks everything from scratch and she has single-handedly cooked for teams of up to 18 shearers. Always conscious to load the food with carbohydrates and proteins, she ensures her daily menu includes pasta, rice puddings, cheese and meat.

"They eat lots of meat. And they eat big quantities, especially at night. During the day, they don't eat so much because they have to bend over all day," she says.

Jenny likes to cook what she calls "good, solid, favourites that everyone likes" and she offers a wide variety at every meal. For dinners, Jenny always provides a three-course meal including soup, roast meat and baked desserts.

"The shearers work so hard. I like to give them good food and they love it."

Shearing and Schedules

The shearing day is long and very regimented. There are usually four shearing 'runs' in a day, and each run lasts for two hours. The only interruptions to the day are the meal times, which are essential for sustaining the shearers during their physically demanding work.

"The daily schedule is strict," Jenny Williams says, *"and the cook has to be on time."*

The typical schedule, and Jenny's daytime menu, looks like this:

7.30am to 9.30am Run One

9.30am Morning Smoko: toasted sandwiches, sausage rolls, quiches, pizzas, lamb roast or ham rolls with gravy followed by cakes, slices and fruit

10am to 12noon Run Two

12noon to 1pm Lunch: cold meats, salads, hot pasta dish (spaghetti bolognaise or lasagne), bread rolls, cakes and slices

1pm to 3pm Run Three

3pm Afternoon tea: lots of fruit from the fridge; sandwiches (corned beef and pickles or salad and ham are popular) and a variety of cakes and slices including the popular favourites chocolate cake, fruitcake and date and walnut loaf.

3.30pm to 5.30pm Run Four

Sunday lunch

A traditional roast, a three-course meal, and a leisurely pace. It's a wise way to spend this day of rest.

CHICKEN AND VEGETABLE SOUP

1.5kg whole chicken

1 small brown onion (80g), halved

2 litres (8 cups) water

5 black peppercorns

2 bay leaves

20g butter

2 trimmed celery stalks (200g), sliced thinly

2 medium carrots (240g), cut into 1cm pieces

1 large potato (300g), cut into 1cm pieces

150g snow peas, trimmed, chopped coarsely

3 green onions, sliced thinly

310g can corn kernels, drained

1 Place chicken, brown onion, the water, peppercorns and bay leaves in large saucepan; bring to the boil. Reduce heat; simmer, covered, 2 hours.

2 Remove chicken from pan. Strain broth through colander into large bowl; discard solids. Allow broth to cool, cover; refrigerate overnight. When chicken is cool enough to handle, remove and discard skin and bones. Shred meat coarsely; cover, refrigerate overnight.

3 Heat butter in same cleaned pan; cook celery, carrot and potato, stirring, until onion softens. Skim and discard fat from surface of broth. Add to pan; bring to the boil. Reduce heat; simmer, covered, about 10 minutes or until vegetables are just tender.

4 Add snow peas, green onion, corn and reserved chicken to soup; cook, covered, 5 minutes or until heated through.

prep and cook time 2 hours 40 minutes (plus refrigeration)
serves 6
nutritional count per serving 9.2g total fat (2.8g saturated fat); 1183kJ (283 cal); 18.8g carbohydrate; 29.1g protein; 4.2g fibre

"I love our late Sunday afternoon family meal. The week is over and it's an interlude before the next week begins."
– Stefano di Pieri

"I can't remember a Sunday when mum didn't have a huge pot of soup simmering on her wood stove and a lamb roast in the oven."
– Wendy Lonnie, Dugay's Bridge, Victoria

ABOVE CREAM OF PUMPKIN SOUP
LEFT POTATO AND LEEK SOUP

CREAM OF PUMPKIN SOUP

40g butter

1 large brown onion (200g), chopped coarsely

3 bacon rashers (210g), chopped coarsely

1.5kg pumpkin, chopped coarsely

2 large potatoes (600g), chopped coarsely

1.25 litres (5 cups) chicken stock

½ cup (125ml) cream

1 Melt butter in large saucepan; cook onion and bacon, stirring, until onion softens. Stir in pumpkin and potato.
2 Stir in stock, bring to the boil; simmer, uncovered, about 20 minutes or until pumpkin is soft.
3 Blend or process soup, in batches, until smooth. Return soup to same cleaned pan, add cream; stir until heated through.

prep and cook time 40 minutes
serves 6
nutritional count per serving 20.9g total fat (12.3g saturated fat); 1555kJ (372 cal); 28g carbohydrate; 16.2g protein; 4.2g fibre

POTATO AND LEEK SOUP

2 medium potatoes (400g), chopped coarsely

2 medium carrots (240g), chopped coarsely

1 large brown onion (200g), chopped coarsely

1 medium tomato (150g), chopped coarsely

1 trimmed celery stalk (100g), chopped coarsely

1.5 litres (6 cups) water

1 tablespoon olive oil

50g butter

4 medium potatoes (800g), chopped coarsely, extra

1 large leek (500g), sliced thickly

300ml cream

2 tablespoons finely chopped fresh chives

1 tablespoon finely chopped fresh basil

1 tablespoon finely chopped fresh dill

1 Combine potato, carrot, onion, tomato, celery and the water in large saucepan; bring to the boil. Reduce heat; simmer, uncovered, 20 minutes. Strain broth through muslin-lined sieve or colander into large heatproof bowl; discard solids.
2 Heat oil and butter in same cleaned pan; cook extra potato and leek, covered, 15 minutes, stirring occasionally. Add broth; bring to the boil. Reduce heat; simmer, covered, 15 minutes. Cool 15 minutes.
3 Blend or process soup, in batches, until smooth. Return soup to same cleaned pan, add cream; stir over medium heat until hot.
4 Serve soup sprinkled with combined herbs and, if desired, topped with croûtons.

prep and cook time 1 hour 20 minutes (plus cooling)
serves 4
nutritional count per serving 47.9g total fat (28.8g saturated fat); 2822kJ (675 cal); 46.3g carbohydrate; 11g protein; 9.8g fibre

sunday lunch

PORK LEG ROAST WITH SAGE POTATOES

You can use boneless pork shoulder roast, if you like.

2.5kg boneless pork leg roast, rind on

2 tablespoons olive oil

1 tablespoon sea salt flakes

6 medium potatoes (1.2kg), quartered

2 tablespoons olive oil, extra

2 tablespoons fresh sage leaves

2 tablespoons fresh rosemary leaves

apple sauce

3 large green apples (600g)

¼ cup (60ml) water

1 teaspoon white sugar

pinch ground cinnamon

1 Preheat oven to 220°C/200°C fan-forced.
2 Score pork rind with sharp knife; rub with oil, then salt. Place pork in large shallow baking dish. Roast, uncovered, 20 minutes.
3 Reduce oven to 180°C/160°C fan-forced. Roast, uncovered, about 2 hours.
4 Meanwhile, combine potato with extra oil and herbs in large bowl. Place in single layer on oven tray. Roast, uncovered, about 35 minutes.
5 Make apple sauce.
6 Stand pork, covered loosely with foil, 10 minutes before slicing. Serve pork and sage potatoes with apple sauce.
apple sauce Peel and core apples; slice thickly. Place apples and the water in medium saucepan; simmer, uncovered, about 10 minutes or until apple is soft. Remove pan from heat; stir in sugar and cinnamon.

prep and cook time 2 hours 40 minutes (plus standing)
serves 8
nutritional count per serving 34g total fat (9.7g saturated fat); 2976kJ (712 cal); 27.4g carbohydrate; 71.9g protein; 4.1g fibre

ROAST LAMB DINNER

2kg lamb leg
3 sprigs fresh rosemary, chopped coarsely
½ teaspoon sweet paprika
1kg potatoes, chopped coarsely
500g piece pumpkin, chopped coarsely
1 large onion (200g), cut into wedges
2 tablespoons olive oil
2 tablespoons plain flour
1 cup (250ml) chicken stock
¼ cup (60ml) dry red wine

mint sauce
¾ cup (180ml) white vinegar
¼ cup (60ml) water
¼ cup (55g) caster sugar
2 cups coarsely chopped fresh mint

cauliflower mornay
1 small cauliflower (1kg), cut into florets
50g butter
¼ cup (35g) plain flour
2 cups (500ml) milk
¾ cup (90g) coarsely grated cheddar cheese

1 Make mint sauce.
2 Meanwhile, preheat oven to 200°C/180°C fan-forced. Place lamb in large oiled baking dish; using sharp knife, score skin at 2cm intervals, sprinkle with rosemary and paprika. Roast, uncovered, 15 minutes.
3 Reduce oven to 180°C/160°C fan-forced. Roast lamb, uncovered, further 45 minutes or until cooked as desired.
4 Meanwhile, place potato, pumpkin and onion, in single layer, in large shallow baking dish; drizzle with oil. Roast, uncovered, for last 45 minutes of lamb cooking time.
5 Make cauliflower mornay.
6 Remove lamb and vegetables from oven; cover to keep warm. Strain pan juices from lamb into medium jug. Return ¼ cup of the pan juices to flameproof dish over medium heat, add flour; cook, stirring, about 5 minutes or until mixture bubbles and browns. Gradually add stock and wine; cook over high heat, stirring, until gravy boils and thickens.
7 Strain gravy; serve with sliced lamb, roasted vegetables, cauliflower mornay and mint sauce.

mint sauce Stir vinegar, the water and sugar in small saucepan over heat, without boiling, until sugar dissolves. Combine vinegar mixture and half of the mint in small heatproof bowl, cover; stand 3 hours. Strain mixture into bowl, discard mint. Stir remaining fresh mint into sauce; blend or process until chopped finely.

cauliflower mornay Boil, steam or microwave cauliflower until tender; drain. Melt butter in medium saucepan, add flour; cook, stirring, until mixture bubbles and thickens. Gradually add milk; cook, stirring, until mixture boils and thickens. Stir in half of the cheese. Preheat grill. Place cauliflower in 1.5-litre (6-cup) shallow flameproof dish; pour sauce over cauliflower, sprinkle with remaining cheese. Place under preheated grill about 10 minutes or until browned lightly.

prep and cook time 2 hours (plus standing)
serves 6
nutritional count per serving 35.6g total fat (17g saturated fat); 3244kJ (776 cal); 40.5g carbohydrate; 71.9g protein; 7g fibre
makes 1 cup mint sauce
nutritional count per tablespoon sauce 0g total fat (0g saturated fat); 96kJ (23 cal); 5g carbohydrate; 0.3g protein; 0.6g fibre

A SUNDAY ROAST IS A MEAL TO BE SAVOURED, ACCOMPANIED BY FAMILY TOGETHERNESS AND CONVERSATION.

"A key ingredient to a good meal is to have the family sitting around the table together."

— Maggie Beer

ABOVE ROAST CHICKEN
LEFT ROASTED ROOT VEGETABLES

ROAST CHICKEN

1.5kg chicken

15g butter, melted

herb stuffing

1½ cups (105g) stale breadcrumbs

1 trimmed celery stalk (100g), chopped finely

1 small white onion (80g), chopped finely

2 teaspoons finely chopped fresh sage leaves

1 tablespoon finely chopped fresh flat-leaf parsley

1 egg, beaten lightly

30g butter, melted

1 Preheat oven to 200°C/180°C fan-forced.
2 Make herb stuffing.
3 Remove and discard any fat from cavity of chicken. Fill cavity of chicken with stuffing, fold over skin to enclose stuffing; secure with toothpicks. Tie legs together with string.
4 Place chicken on rack over baking dish. Half-fill baking dish with water – it should not touch the chicken. Brush chicken with butter; roast 15 minutes.
5 Reduce oven 180°C/160°C fan-forced. Bake further 1½ hours or until chicken is cooked through, basting occasionally with pan juices. Stand 10 minutes before breaking or cutting into serving-sized pieces.
herb stuffing Combine ingredients in medium bowl.

prep and cook time 2 hours 15 minutes
serves 4
nutritional count per serving 35.9g total fat (14.4g saturated fat); 2437kJ (583 cal); 19.4g carbohydrate; 45g protein; 1.9g fibre

ROASTED ROOT VEGETABLES

2 tablespoons olive oil

12 baby carrots (240g), peeled, halved lengthways

3 small parsnips (180g), peeled, quartered lengthways

12 baby potatoes (480g), halved

4 baby onions (100g), halved

1 clove garlic, crushed

1 tablespoon coarsely chopped fresh rosemary sprigs

1 tablespoon honey

2 teaspoons seeded mustard

1 tablespoon lemon juice

1 Preheat oven to 220°C/200°C fan-forced.
2 Heat oil in large flameproof baking dish; cook carrot, parsnip, potato and onion, stirring, until browned lightly. Remove from heat; stir in garlic, rosemary, honey and mustard.
3 Bake about 25 minutes or until vegetables are tender. Serve drizzled with lemon juice.

prep and cook time 50 minutes
serves 4
nutritional count per serving 4.9g total fat (0.6g saturated fat); 798kJ (191 cal); 29.3g carbohydrate; 4.5g protein; 5.3g fibre

sunday lunch

100

the *country* table

"Good food should be an experience: it doesn't have to be fancy. It should just evoke something and speak of something. And it should be about using the food of place."
– Stefano di Pieri

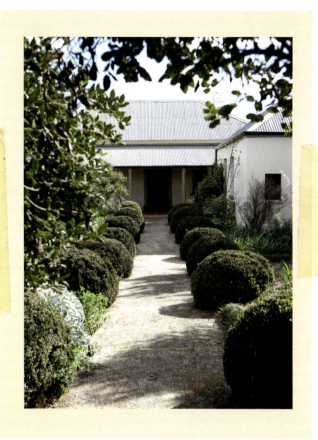

LAMB SHANK STEW

8 french-trimmed lamb shanks (1.6kg)

8 cloves garlic, halved

2 medium lemons (280g)

2 tablespoons olive oil

3 large brown onions (600g), chopped coarsely

2 cups (500ml) dry red wine

3 medium carrots (360g), quartered lengthways

3 trimmed celery stalks (300g), chopped coarsely

4 bay leaves

8 sprigs fresh thyme

1.75 litres (7 cups) chicken stock

½ cup finely chopped fresh flat-leaf parsley

¼ cup finely chopped fresh mint

2kg potatoes, chopped coarsely

300ml cream

100g butter

1 Pierce meatiest part of each shank in two places with sharp knife; press garlic into cuts.
2 Grate rind of both lemons finely; reserve. Halve lemons; rub cut sides all over shanks.
3 Preheat oven to 180°C/160°C fan-forced.
4 Heat oil in large flameproof casserole dish; cook shanks, in batches, over heat until browned. Cook onion, stirring, in same dish until softened. Add wine; bring to the boil, then remove dish from heat.
5 Place carrot, celery and shanks, in alternate layers, on onion mixture in dish. Top with bay leaves and thyme; carefully pour stock over the top. Cover dish tightly with lid or foil; cook in oven about 3 hours or until meat is tender.
6 Combine reserved grated rind and herbs in bowl.
7 Boil, steam or microwave potato until tender; drain. Mash potato with warmed cream and butter in large bowl until smooth. Cover to keep warm.
8 Transfer shanks to platter; cover to keep warm. Strain pan juices through muslin-lined sieve into medium saucepan; discard solids. Boil pan juices, uncovered, stirring occasionally, until reduced by half.
9 Divide mashed potato among plates; top with shanks, sprinkle with rind-herb mixture, drizzle with pan juices. Serve with green beans, if desired.

prep and cook time 3 hours 20 minutes *serves* 8
nutritional count per serving 34.3g total fat (19.5g saturated fat); 2721kJ (651 cal); 37.8g carbohydrate; 34.3g protein; 7.4g fibre

ABOVE STANDING RIB ROAST WITH ROAST VEGETABLES
LEFT BEEF AND VEGETABLE PIE

STANDING RIB ROAST WITH ROAST VEGETABLES

1.2kg beef standing rib roast

¼ cup (60ml) olive oil

2 teaspoons cracked black pepper

500g tiny new potatoes

500g pumpkin, chopped coarsely

500g kumara, chopped coarsely

½ cup (125ml) brandy

1½ cups (375ml) beef stock

1 tablespoon cornflour

¼ cup (60ml) water

1 tablespoon finely chopped fresh chives

1 Preheat oven to 200°C/180°C fan-forced.
2 Brush beef with 1 tablespoon of the oil; sprinkle with pepper. Heat 1 tablespoon of the oil in large shallow flameproof baking dish; cook beef, uncovered, over high heat until browned all over. Roast, uncovered, in oven about 45 minutes or until cooked as desired.
3 Meanwhile, heat remaining oil in another large flameproof baking dish; cook potatoes, stirring, over high heat until browned lightly. Add pumpkin and kumara, place dish in oven with beef; roast, uncovered, about 35 minutes or until vegetables are browned.
4 Place beef on vegetables, cover; return to oven to keep warm. Drain juices from beef baking dish into medium saucepan, add brandy; bring to the boil. Add stock and blended cornflour and water; cook, stirring, until sauce boils and thickens slightly. Stir in chives; pour into medium heatproof jug.
5 Serve beef and vegetables with sauce.

prep and cook time 1 hour 50 minutes
serves 4
nutritional count per serving 29.2g total fat (8.5g saturated fat); 3114kJ (745 cal); 41.1g carbohydrate; 60.4g protein; 5.4g fibre

BEEF AND VEGETABLE PIE

1 tablespoon olive oil

1.5kg gravy beef, cut into 2cm pieces

60g butter

1 medium brown onion (150g), chopped finely

1 clove garlic, crushed

¼ cup (35g) plain flour

1 cup (250ml) dry white wine

3 cups (750ml) hot beef stock

2 tablespoons tomato paste

2 trimmed celery stalks (200g), cut into 2cm pieces

2 medium potatoes (400g), cut into 2cm pieces

1 large carrot (180g), cut into 2cm pieces

1 large zucchini (150g), cut into 2cm pieces

150g mushrooms, quartered

1 cup (120g) frozen peas

½ cup finely chopped fresh flat-leaf parsley

2 sheets ready-rolled puff pastry

1 egg, beaten lightly

1 Heat oil in large saucepan; cook beef, in batches, until browned all over.
2 Melt butter in same pan; cook onion and garlic, stirring, until onion softens. Add flour; cook, stirring, until mixture bubbles and thickens. Stir in wine and stock; stir until mixture boils and thickens slightly.
3 Return beef to pan with paste, celery, potato and carrot; bring to the boil. Reduce heat; simmer, covered, 1 hour. Add zucchini and mushrooms; simmer, uncovered, about 30 minutes or until beef is tender. Add peas; stir until heated through. Remove from heat; stir in parsley.
4 Preheat oven to 220°C/200°C fan-forced.
5 Divide warm beef mixture between two deep 25cm pie dishes; brush edge of dishes with a little egg. Top each with a pastry sheet; pressing edges to seal. Trim; brush pastry with egg. Bake 20 minutes or until browned.

prep and cook time 2 hours 40 minutes *serves* 8
nutritional count per serving 27.6g total fat (13.3g saturated fat); 2412kJ (577 cal); 28.6g carbohydrate; 46.4g protein; 4.9g fibre

"We have a close connection to the source of our food and we really embrace seasonality. Meals in the country are all about sharing, conviviality and the freshest, tastiest produce in the tradition of slow food."

– Trisha Dixon, Cooma, New South Wales

"There is nothing better than sharing the table with family and friends – with visitors from the city – and eating together with no formality."
– Stefano di Pieri

ABOVE RHUBARB AND PEAR SPONGE PUDDING
LEFT LEMON DELICIOUS PUDDING

RHUBARB AND PEAR SPONGE PUDDING

825g can pear slices in natural juice

800g rhubarb, trimmed, cut into 4cm pieces

2 tablespoons caster sugar

2 eggs

⅓ cup (75g) caster sugar, extra

2 tablespoons plain flour

2 tablespoons self-raising flour

2 tablespoons cornflour

1 Preheat oven to 180°C/160°C fan-forced.
2 Drain pears; reserve ¾ cup (180ml) of the juice.
3 Place reserved juice, rhubarb and sugar in large saucepan; cook, stirring occasionally, about 5 minutes or until rhubarb is just tender. Stir in pears. Pour mixture into deep 1.75-litre (7-cup) ovenproof dish.
4 Meanwhile, beat eggs in small bowl with electric mixer until thick and creamy. Gradually add extra sugar, 1 tablespoon at a time, beating until sugar dissolves between additions. Gently fold in combined sifted flours.
5 Spread sponge mixture over hot rhubarb mixture. Bake about 45 minutes or until browned lightly and cooked through.

prep and cook time 1 hour 10 minutes
serves 6
nutritional count per serving 2.1g total fat (0.6g saturated fat); 823kJ (197 cal); 35.7g carbohydrate; 5.4g protein; 5.9g fibre

LEMON DELICIOUS PUDDING

125g butter, melted

2 teaspoons finely grated lemon rind

1½ cups (330g) caster sugar

3 eggs, separated

½ cup (75g) self-raising flour

⅓ cup (80ml) lemon juice

1⅓ cups (330ml) milk

1 Preheat oven to 180°C/160°C fan-forced. Grease six 1-cup (250ml) ovenproof dishes.
2 Combine butter, rind, sugar and yolks in large bowl. Stir in sifted flour then juice. Gradually stir in milk; mixture should be smooth and runny.
3 Beat egg whites in small bowl with electric mixer until soft peaks form; fold into lemon mixture, in two batches.
4 Place ovenproof dishes in large baking dish; divide lemon mixture among dishes. Add enough boiling water to baking dish to come halfway up sides of ovenproof dishes. Bake, uncovered, about 45 minutes.

prep and cook time 1 hour
serves 6
nutritional count per serving 22g total fat (13.5g saturated fat); 2069kJ (495 cal); 67.1g carbohydrate; 6.7g protein; 0.5g fibre

OLD-FASHIONED APPLE PIE

8 medium (1.5kg) apples
⅔ cup (150g) caster sugar
½ cup (125ml) water
2 tablespoons white sugar, optional

pastry
3 cups (450g) self-raising flour
¼ cup (40g) icing sugar
125g cold butter, chopped coarsely
1 egg, beaten lightly
½ cup (125ml) milk, approximately

passionfruit icing
1½ cups (240g) icing sugar
2 passionfruit

1 Peel, quarter and core apples; slice thickly. Place apples, caster sugar and the water in large saucepan; cover, bring to the boil, reduce heat, simmer about 10 minutes or until the apples are just tender. Gently turn the apple mixture into a large colander or strainer to drain; cool to room temperature.
2 Preheat oven to 200°C/180°C fan-forced. Grease 20cm x 30cm lamington pan; line base with baking paper, extending paper 5cm over two long sides.
3 Make pastry.
4 Roll two-thirds of the pastry on floured surface until large enough to line base and sides of pan, with 1cm extending over sides. Lift pastry into pan. Spread cold apple mixture into pastry case; brush edges with a little extra milk. Roll out remaining pastry until large enough to generously cover pie. Place over filling; press edges together to seal. Trim excess pastry around edges. Brush top with a little milk; sprinkle with white sugar. Slash about six holes in pastry.
5 Bake pie 45 minutes. Stand in pan 10 minutes; turn, right-side up, on wire rack to cool.
6 Meanwhile, make passionfruit icing. Spread icing over pastry; serve cut into squares.

pastry Sift flour and icing sugar into large bowl; rub in butter. Make a well in centre. Using a knife, 'cut' combined egg and enough milk through flour mixture to make a soft dough.

passionfruit icing Sift icing sugar into medium heatproof bowl, stir in passionfruit pulp, then enough water to make a stiff paste. Place bowl over saucepan of simmering water; stir icing until spreadable.

prep and cook time 1 hour 40 minutes (plus cooling)
serves 8
nutritional count per serving 14.9g total fat (9.2g saturated fat); 2658kJ (636 cal); 114.1g carbohydrate; 7.6g protein; 5.3g fibre

"I love the idea of inheriting recipes and making desserts that my mother, grandmother and other relatives have made before me."
– Fiona Slack-Smith, Mudgee, New South Wales

NOTE NUTMEG IS A VERY PUNGENT SPICE GROUND FROM THE NUT OF AN INDONESIAN EVERGREEN TREE. USUALLY PURCHASED GROUND, THE FLAVOUR IS MORE INTENSE IF YOU GRATE IT FRESH FROM THE WHOLE NUT, WHICH IS AVAILABLE FROM SPICE SHOPS.

TOP LEFT RICE PUDDING
ABOVE STEAMED GINGER PUDDING

RICE PUDDING

½ cup (100g) uncooked white medium-grain rice

2½ cups (625ml) milk

¼ cup (55g) caster sugar

¼ cup (40g) sultanas

½ teaspoon vanilla extract

2 teaspoons butter

½ teaspoon ground nutmeg

1 Preheat oven to 160°C/140°C fan-forced. Grease shallow 1-litre (4-cup) baking dish.
2 Wash rice under cold water; drain well. Place rice, milk, sugar, sultanas and extract in dish; whisk lightly with fork. Dot with butter.
3 Bake rice, uncovered, 1 hour, whisking lightly with fork under skin occasionally. Sprinkle with nutmeg; bake further 20 minutes. Serve warm or cold.

prep and cook time 1 hour 20 minutes
serves 6
nutritional count per serving 5.5g total fat (3.6g saturated fat); 840kJ (201 cal); 32.4g carbohydrate; 4.8g protein; 0.4g fibre

STEAMED GINGER PUDDING

60g butter

¼ cup (90g) golden syrup

½ teaspoon bicarbonate of soda

1 cup (150g) self-raising flour

2 teaspoons ground ginger

½ cup (125ml) milk

1 egg

syrup

⅓ cup (115g) golden syrup

2 tablespoons water

30g butter

1 Grease 1.25-litre (5-cup) pudding steamer.
2 Stir butter and syrup in small saucepan over low heat until smooth. Remove from heat, stir in soda; transfer mixture to medium bowl. Stir in sifted dry ingredients then combined milk and egg, in two batches.
3 Spread mixture into steamer. Cover with pleated baking paper and foil; secure with lid.
4 Place pudding steamer in large saucepan with enough boiling water to come halfway up side of steamer; cover pan with tight-fitting lid. Boil 1 hour, replenishing water as necessary to maintain level. Stand pudding 5 minutes; turn onto plate.
5 Meanwhile, make syrup.
6 Serve steamed pudding topped with syrup and, if desired, cream.
syrup Stir ingredients in small saucepan over heat until smooth; bring to the boil. Reduce heat; simmer, uncovered, 2 minutes.

prep and cook time 1 hour 15 minutes
serves 6
nutritional count per serving 14.3g total fat (9g saturated fat); 1367kJ (327 cal); 44.5g carbohydrate; 4.5g protein; 1g fibre

SPICED APRICOT AND PLUM PIE

2 x 825g cans dark plums in light syrup
2 cups (300g) dried apricots
1 cinnamon stick
3 cloves
½ teaspoon mixed spice
½ teaspoon ground ginger
2 sheets ready-rolled puff pastry
1 egg, beaten lightly
icing sugar, for dusting

spiced yogurt cream
½ cup (140g) natural yogurt
½ cup (120g) sour cream
1 tablespoon ground cinnamon
¼ teaspoon ground ginger

1 Preheat oven to 200°C/180°C fan-forced. Grease deep 1.25 litre (5-cup) rectangular dish or 26cm pie dish.
2 Drain plums; reserve 1 cup of the syrup. Halve plums, discard stones; place plums in dish.
3 Combine reserved syrup, apricots, cinnamon, cloves, mixed spice and ginger in medium saucepan; simmer, uncovered, until liquid is reduced to ½ cup. Remove and discard cinnamon stick and cloves; cool to room temperature. Pour mixture over plums.
4 Cut pastry into 2.5cm strips. Brush edges of dish with a little of the egg; press pastry strips around edges of dish. Twist remaining strips, place over filling in a lattice pattern; trim ends, brush top with remaining egg.
5 Bake pie about 40 minutes or until pastry is browned lightly.
6 Make spiced yogurt cream.
7 Dust pie generously with icing sugar; serve with spiced yogurt cream.
spiced yogurt cream Combine ingredients in small bowl.

prep and cook time 1 hour 10 minutes (plus cooling)
serves 8
nutritional count per serving 16.9g total fat (9.6g saturated fat); 1751kJ (419 cal); 57.1g carbohydrate; 6.4g protein; 6.3g fibre

sunday lunch

See you at three

It's good to know you can always rely on your friends and the gentle art of freshly-baked afternoon tea.

DUTCH GINGER AND ALMOND SLICE

1¾ cups (255g) plain flour

1 cup (220g) caster sugar

⅔ cup (150g) coarsely chopped glacé ginger

½ cup (80g) blanched almonds, chopped coarsely

1 egg

185g butter, melted

2 teaspoons icing sugar

1 Preheat oven to 180°C/160°C fan-forced. Line 20cm x 30cm lamington pan with baking paper, extending paper 2cm over long sides.
2 Combine flour, sugar, ginger, nuts and egg in medium bowl; stir in butter. Press mixture into pan.
3 Bake slice about 35 minutes. Stand in pan 10 minutes; lift onto wire rack to cool. Dust with sifted icing sugar before cutting.

prep and cook time 50 minutes
makes 20
nutritional count per piece 10.2g total fat (5.2g saturated fat); 861kJ (206 cal); 25.8g carbohydrate; 2.4g protein; 0.8g fibre

"Country people are renowned for their warm hospitality. The cake tins always have several offerings at the ready for when unexpected guests pop in for a cuppa."
– Pamela Clark

ABOVE DATE SLICE
LEFT TANGY LEMON SQUARES

DATE SLICE

1½ cups (225g) plain flour
1¼ cups (185g) self-raising flour
150g cold butter, chopped
1 tablespoon honey
1 egg
⅓ cup (80ml) milk, approximately
2 teaspoons milk, extra
1 tablespoon white sugar

date filling
3½ cups (500g) dried seeded dates, chopped coarsely
¾ cup (180ml) water
2 tablespoons finely grated lemon rind
2 tablespoons lemon juice

1 Grease 20cm x 30cm lamington pan; line base with baking paper, extending paper 5cm over long sides.
2 Sift flours into large bowl; rub in butter until mixture is crumbly. Stir in combined honey and egg and enough milk to make a firm dough. Knead on floured surface until smooth. Cover; refrigerate 30 minutes.
3 Meanwhile, make date filling.
4 Preheat oven to 200°C/180°C fan-forced.
5 Divide dough in half. Roll one half large enough to cover base of pan; press into pan, spread filling over dough. Roll remaining dough large enough to cover filling. Brush with extra milk; sprinkle with sugar. Bake about 20 minutes; cool in pan.
date filling Cook ingredients in medium saucepan, stirring, about 10 minutes or until thick and smooth. Cool to room temperature.

prep and cook time 1 hour 25 minutes (plus refrigeration)
makes 24
nutritional count per piece 5.7g total fat (3.6g saturated fat); 757kJ (181 cal); 28.2g carbohydrate;

TANGY LEMON SQUARES

125g butter
¼ cup (40g) icing sugar
1¼ cups (185g) plain flour
3 eggs
1 cup (220g) caster sugar
2 teaspoons finely grated lemon rind
½ cup (125ml) lemon juice

1 Preheat oven to 180°C/160°C fan-forced. Grease shallow 23cm-square pan; line base and sides of pan with baking paper, extending paper 2cm above edges of pan.
2 Beat butter and icing sugar in small bowl with electric mixer until smooth. Stir in 1 cup (150g) of the flour. Press mixture evenly over base of pan.
3 Bake base about 15 minutes or until browned lightly.
4 Meanwhile, whisk eggs, caster sugar, remaining flour, rind and juice in bowl until combined. Pour egg mixture over hot base.
5 Bake slice about 20 minutes or until firm. Cool in pan on a wire rack before cutting. Dust with extra sifted icing sugar, if desired.

prep and cook time 50 minutes
makes 16
nutritional count per piece 7.5g total fat (4.5g saturated fat); 748kJ (179 cal); 24.9g carbohydrate; 2.6g protein; 0.5g fibre

122

the *country* table

"There's no lack of good food out here. I jump in the ute and go for coffee and cake at the neighbours'."
– Robyn Blanchett, Wagin, Western Australia

ABOVE HEDGEHOG SLICE
LEFT RASPBERRY COCONUT SLICE

HEDGEHOG SLICE

¾ cup (180ml) sweetened condensed milk

60g butter

125g dark eating chocolate, chopped coarsely

150g plain sweet biscuits

⅓ cup (45g) roasted unsalted peanuts

⅓ cup (55g) sultanas

1 Grease 8cm x 26cm bar pan; line base with baking paper, extending paper 5cm over long sides.
2 Stir condensed milk and butter in small saucepan over low heat until smooth. Remove from heat; add chocolate, stir until smooth.
3 Break biscuits into small pieces; place biscuits in large bowl with nuts and sultanas. Add chocolate mixture; stir to combine.
4 Spread mixture into pan. Cover; refrigerate about 4 hours or until firm. Remove from pan; cut into squares.

prep and cook time 15 minutes (plus refrigeration)
makes 12
nutritional count per piece 12.7g total fat (6.9g saturated fat); 1053kJ (252 cal); 30g carbohydrate; 4g protein; 0.9g fibre

RASPBERRY COCONUT SLICE

90g butter

½ cup (110g) caster sugar

1 egg

¼ cup (35g) self-raising flour

⅔ cup (100g) plain flour

1 tablespoon custard powder

⅔ cup (220g) raspberry jam

coconut topping

2 cups (160g) desiccated coconut

¼ cup (55g) caster sugar

2 eggs, beaten lightly

1 Preheat oven to 180°C/160°C fan-forced. Grease 20cm x 30cm lamington pan; line base with baking paper, extending paper 5cm over long sides.
2 Beat butter, sugar and egg in small bowl with electric mixer until light and fluffy. Transfer to medium bowl; stir in sifted flours and custard powder. Spread dough into pan; spread with jam.
3 Make coconut topping; sprinkle topping over jam.
4 Bake slice about 40 minutes; cool in pan.
coconut topping Combine ingredients in small bowl.

prep and cook time 1 hour (plus cooling)
makes 16
nutritional count per piece 11.6g total fat (8.9g saturated fat); 932kJ (223 cal); 26.7g carbohydrate; 2g protein; 2g fibre

HUMMINGBIRD CAKE

You need approximately 2 large overripe bananas (460g) for this recipe.

450g can crushed pineapple in syrup

1 cup (150g) plain flour

½ cup (75g) self-raising flour

½ teaspoon bicarbonate of soda

½ teaspoon ground cinnamon

½ teaspoon ground ginger

1 cup (200g) firmly packed brown sugar

½ cup (45g) desiccated coconut

1 cup mashed banana

2 eggs, beaten lightly

¾ cup (180ml) vegetable oil

cream cheese frosting

30g butter, softened

60g cream cheese, softened

1 teaspoon vanilla extract

1½ cups (240g) icing sugar

1 Preheat oven to 180°C/160°C fan-forced. Grease deep 23cm-square cake pan, line base with baking paper.
2 Drain pineapple over medium bowl, pressing with spoon to extract as much syrup as possible. Reserve ¼ cup (60ml) syrup.
3 Sift flours, soda, spices and sugar into large bowl. Using wooden spoon, stir in drained pineapple, reserved syrup, coconut, banana, egg and oil; pour into pan.
4 Bake cake about 40 minutes. Stand in pan 5 minutes; turn, top-side up, on wire rack to cool.
5 Meanwhile, make cream cheese frosting. Spread cold cake with frosting.
cream cheese frosting Beat butter, cream cheese and extract in small bowl with electric mixer until light and fluffy; gradually beat in icing sugar.

prep and cook time 1 hour 10 minutes
serves 12
nutritional count per serving 21.1g total fat (6.6g saturated fat); 1881kJ (450 cal); 59.5g carbohydrate; 4.5g protein; 2.2g fibre

THIS MOIST, LUSCIOUS CAKE FROM THE AMERICAN DEEP SOUTH TRANSLATES AS DELICIOUS IN ANYONE'S LANGUAGE. MAKE SURE YOU DRAIN THE PINEAPPLE THOROUGHLY FOR THIS RECIPE OTHERWISE THE CAKE WILL BE SOGGY.

TIP A SPONGE COOKS BEST WHEN THE TOP OF EACH PAN IS IN THE CENTRE OF THE OVEN. IF PANS ARE ON DIFFERENT SHELVES, SWAP THEM AROUND HALFWAY THROUGH BAKING SO SPONGES COOK EVENLY.

TOP LEFT ECONOMICAL BOILED FRUIT CAKE
LEFT FEATHERLIGHT SPONGE CAKE

ECONOMICAL BOILED FRUIT CAKE

2¾ cups (500g) mixed dried fruit

1 cup (220g) firmly packed brown sugar

125g butter, chopped

½ cup (125ml) water

1 teaspoon mixed spice

½ teaspoon bicarbonate of soda

½ cup (125ml) sweet sherry

1 egg

1 cup (150g) plain flour

1 cup (150g) self-raising flour

⅓ cup (55g) blanched almonds

2 tablespoons sweet sherry, extra

1 Stir fruit, sugar, butter, the water, spice and soda in large saucepan over low heat, without boiling, until sugar dissolves and butter melts; bring to the boil. Reduce heat; simmer, covered, 5 minutes. Remove from heat; stir in sherry. Cool to room temperature.
2 Preheat oven to 160°C/140°C fan-forced. Grease deep 20cm-round cake pan; line base and side with two layers of baking paper, extending paper 5cm above side.
3 Stir egg and sifted flours into fruit mixture. Spread mixture into pan; decorate with almonds.
4 Bake cake about 1½ hours. Brush top of hot cake with extra sherry. Cover cake with foil; cool in pan.

prep and cook time 1 hour 45 minutes (plus cooling)
serves 12
nutritional count per serving 12.2g total fat (6.1g saturated fat); 1718kJ (411 cal); 64.6g carbohydrate; 5g protein; 3.7g fibre

FEATHERLIGHT SPONGE CAKE

4 eggs

¾ cup (165g) caster sugar

⅔ cup (100g) wheaten cornflour

¼ cup (30g) custard powder

1 teaspoon cream of tartar

½ teaspoon bicarbonate of soda

⅓ cup (110g) apricot jam

300ml thickened cream, whipped

1 Preheat oven to 180°C/160°C fan-forced. Grease and flour two deep 22cm-round cake pans.
2 Beat eggs and sugar in small bowl with electric mixer until thick, creamy and sugar dissolved. Transfer mixture to large bowl; fold in triple-sifted dry ingredients. Divide mixture between pans.
3 Bake sponges about 20 minutes. Turn, top-side up, onto baking-paper-covered wire rack to cool.
4 Sandwich sponges with jam and cream.

prep and cook time 40 minutes
serves 10
nutritional count per serving 13.3g total fat (8g saturated fat); 1195kJ (286 cal); 37.2g carbohydrate; 3.8g protein; 0.7g fibre

"Some of the best bakers in the nation are country cooks. Baking in the country is about community and getting together and bringing a plate."
– Maggie Beer

PATTY CAKES WITH GLACÉ ICING

125g butter, softened
1 teaspoon vanilla extract
⅔ cup (150g) caster sugar
3 eggs
1½ cups (225g) self-raising flour
¼ cup (60ml) milk
glacé icing
1½ cups (240g) icing sugar
1 teaspoon butter
2 tablespoons milk, approximately

1 Preheat oven to 180°C/160°C fan-forced. Line two deep 12-hole patty pans with paper cases.
2 Beat butter, extract, sugar, eggs, flour and milk in medium bowl with electric mixer at low speed until just combined. Increase speed to medium; beat about 3 minutes or until mixture is smooth and paler in colour. Drop slightly rounded tablespoons of mixture into paper cases.
3 Bake cakes about 20 minutes. Turn, top-side up, onto wire racks to cool.
4 Meanwhile, make glacé icing; top cakes with icing.
glacé icing Sift icing sugar into small heatproof bowl; stir in butter and enough milk to give a firm paste. Set bowl over small saucepan of simmering water; stir until icing is spreadable.

prep and cook time 40 minutes (plus cooling)
makes 24
nutritional count per patty cake 5.4g total fat (3.2g saturated fat); 627kJ (150 cal); 23.1g carbohydrate; 1.9g protein; 0.4g fibre

"Home-baked afternoon tea is the perfect punctuation in a long afternoon. It carries you through to dinner."
– Claire MacTaggart, Rockhampton, Queensland

LAMINGTONS

6 eggs
⅔ cup (150g) caster sugar
⅓ cup (50g) cornflour
½ cup (75g) plain flour
⅓ cup (50g) self-raising flour
2 cups (160g) desiccated coconut
icing
4 cups (640g) icing sugar
½ cup (50g) cocoa powder
15g butter, melted
1 cup (250ml) milk

1 Preheat oven to 180°C/160°C fan-forced. Grease 20cm x 30cm lamington pan; line with baking paper, extending paper 5cm over long sides.
2 Beat eggs in large bowl with electric mixer about 10 minutes or until thick and creamy; gradually beat in sugar, dissolving between additions. Fold in triple-sifted flours. Spread mixture into pan.
3 Bake cake about 35 minutes. Turn immediately onto baking-paper-covered wire rack to cool.
4 Meanwhile, make icing.
5 Cut cake into 16 squares; dip each piece in icing, drain off excess. Toss squares in coconut. Place lamingtons onto wire rack to set.
icing Sift icing sugar and cocoa into medium heatproof bowl; stir in butter and milk. Place bowl over medium saucepan of simmering water; stir until icing is of a coating consistency.

prep and cook time 50 minutes
makes 16
nutritional count per lamington 10.4g total fat (1.8g saturated fat); 1501kJ (359 cal); 59.6g carbohydrate; 5.1g protein; 1.9g fibre

VARIATION: PINK JELLY CAKES
MAKE 80G PACKET OF STRAWBERRY JELLY AS PER PACKET INSTRUCTIONS. REFRIGERATE UNTIL SET TO CONSISTENCY OF UNBEATEN EGG WHITE. DIP CAKE SQUARES INTO JELLY THEN DESICCATED COCONUT. BEAT 300ML THICKENED CREAM UNTIL FIRM PEAKS FORM. HALVE CAKES HORIZONTALLY; SANDWICH CAKES WITH WHIPPED CREAM.

ABOVE BOILED CHOCOLATE CAKE
LEFT ORANGE CAKE

136

the *country* table

BOILED CHOCOLATE CAKE

3 cups (660g) caster sugar

250g butter, chopped

2 cups (500ml) water

⅓ cup (35g) cocoa powder

1 teaspoon bicarbonate of soda

3 cups (450g) self-raising flour

4 eggs

fudge frosting

90g butter

½ cup (110g) caster sugar

⅓ cup (80ml) water

1½ cups (240g) icing sugar

⅓ cup (35g) cocoa powder

1 Preheat oven to 180°C/160°C fan-forced. Grease deep 26.5cm x 33cm (3.5-litre/14-cup) baking dish; line base with baking paper.
2 Stir sugar, butter, the water and sifted cocoa and soda in medium saucepan over heat, without boiling, until sugar dissolves; bring to the boil. Reduce heat; simmer, uncovered, 5 minutes. Transfer mixture to large bowl; cool to room temperature.
3 Add flour and eggs to bowl; beat with electric mixer until mixture is smooth and pale in colour. Pour mixture into pan.
4 Bake cake about 50 minutes. Stand in pan 10 minutes; turn, top-side up, onto wire rack to cool.
5 Meanwhile, make fudge frosting. Spread cold cake with frosting.
fudge frosting Stir butter, caster sugar and the water in small saucepan over low heat, without boiling, until sugar dissolves. Sift icing sugar and cocoa into small bowl then gradually stir in hot butter mixture. Cover; refrigerate about 20 minutes or until frosting thickens. Beat with wooden spoon until spreadable.

prep and cook time 1 hour 10 minutes (plus cooling)
serves 20
nutritional count per serving 15.8g total fat (9.8g saturated fat); 1806kJ (432 cal); 67.3g carbohydrate; 4.3g protein; 1g fibre

ORANGE CAKE

150g butter, softened

1 tablespoon finely grated orange rind

⅔ cup (150g) caster sugar

3 eggs

1½ cups (225g) self-raising flour

¼ cup (60ml) milk

¾ cup (120g) icing sugar

1½ tablespoons orange juice

1 Preheat oven to 180°C/160°C fan-forced. Grease deep 20cm-round cake pan.
2 Beat butter, rind, caster sugar, eggs, flour and milk in medium bowl with electric mixer at low speed until just combined. Increase speed to medium, beat about 3 minutes or until mixture is smooth. Spread mixture into pan.
3 Bake cake about 40 minutes. Stand in pan 5 minutes; turn, top-side up, onto wire rack to cool.
4 Combine sifted icing sugar and juice in small bowl; spread over cake.

prep and cook time 50 minutes
serves 12
nutritional count per serving 12g total fat (7.3g saturated fat); 1129kJ (270 cal); 36.4g carbohydrate; 3.8g protein; 0.7g fibre

see you at three

CINNAMON TEACAKE

60g butter, softened

1 teaspoon vanilla extract

⅔ cup (150g) caster sugar

1 egg

1 cup (150g) self-raising flour

⅓ cup (80ml) milk

10g butter, melted, extra

1 teaspoon ground cinnamon

1 tablespoon caster sugar, extra

1 Preheat oven to 180°C/160°C fan-forced. Grease deep 20cm-round cake pan; line base with baking paper.
2 Beat butter, extract, sugar and egg in small bowl with electric mixer until light and fluffy, this will take about 10 minutes. Stir in sifted flour and milk. Spread mixture into pan.
3 Bake cake about 30 minutes. Turn cake onto wire rack then turn top-side up; brush top with extra butter, sprinkle with combined cinnamon and extra sugar. Serve warm with butter, if desired.

prep and cook time 45 minutes
serves 10
nutritional count per serving 6.8g total fat (4.2g saturated fat); 769kJ (184 cal); 27.8g carbohydrate; 2.5g protein; 0.6g fibre

TAKING CARE TO THOROUGHLY BEAT THE BUTTER, ESSENCE, SUGAR AND EGG WILL RESULT IN A LIGHT-AS-AIR TEXTURE TO THIS CAKE, BEST WHEN EATEN WARM WITH BUTTER

"It's the camaraderie. Friends, home-made cake, flowers from the garden and too much laughing. It all goes together."
— Robyn Blanchett, Wagin, Western Australia

ABOVE BANANA CAKE WITH PASSIONFRUIT ICING
LEFT CARROT CAKE WITH LEMON CREAM CHEESE FROSTING

BANANA CAKE WITH PASSIONFRUIT ICING

You need approximately 2 large overripe bananas (460g) for this recipe and 2 large passionfruit.

125g butter, softened

¾ cup (165g) firmly packed brown sugar

2 eggs

1½ cups (225g) self-raising flour

½ teaspoon bicarbonate of soda

1 teaspoon mixed spice

1 cup mashed banana

½ cup (120g) sour cream

¼ cup (60ml) milk

passionfruit icing

1½ cups (240g) icing sugar

1 teaspoon soft butter

2 tablespoons passionfruit pulp, approximately

1 Preheat oven to 180°C/160°C fan-forced. Grease 15cm x 25cm loaf pan; line base with baking paper.
2 Beat butter and sugar in small bowl with electric mixer until light and fluffy; beat in eggs, one at a time. Transfer to large bowl; stir in sifted dry ingredients, banana, sour cream and milk. Spread mixture into pan.
3 Bake cake about 50 minutes. Stand in pan 5 minutes; turn, top-side up, onto wire rack to cool.
4 Meanwhile, make passionfruit icing. Spread cake with icing.
passionfruit icing Combine ingredients in medium bowl.

prep and cook time 1 hour 25 minutes (plus cooling)
serves 10
nutritional count per serving 17g total fat (10.7g saturated fat); 1768kJ (423 cal); 61.5g carbohydrate; 4.7g protein; 1.9g fibre

CARROT CAKE WITH LEMON CREAM CHEESE FROSTING

You need approximately 3 large carrots (540g) for this recipe.

3 eggs

1⅓ cups (250g) firmly packed brown sugar

1 cup (250ml) vegetable oil

3 cups firmly packed, coarsely grated carrot

1 cup (120g) coarsely chopped walnuts

2½ cups (375g) self-raising flour

½ teaspoon bicarbonate of soda

2 teaspoons mixed spice

lemon cream cheese frosting

30g butter, softened

80g cream cheese, softened

1 teaspoon finely grated lemon rind

1½ cups (240g) icing sugar

1 Preheat oven to 180°C/160°C fan-forced. Grease deep 22cm-round cake pan, line base with baking paper.
2 Beat eggs, sugar and oil in small bowl with electric mixer until thick and creamy. Transfer mixture to large bowl; stir in carrot and nuts then sifted dry ingredients. Pour mixture into pan.
3 Bake cake about 1¼ hours. Stand in pan 5 minutes; turn, top-side up, onto wire rack to cool.
4 Meanwhile, make lemon cream cheese frosting. Spread cold cake with frosting.
lemon cream cheese frosting Beat butter, cream cheese and rind in small bowl with electric mixer until light and fluffy; gradually beat in icing sugar.

prep and cook time 1 hour 25 minutes
serves 12
nutritional count per serving 32.1g total fat (6.1g saturated fat); 2416kJ (578 cal); 64.2g carbohydrate; 7g protein; 2.7g fibre

best in show

COMPETITION IS ALWAYS FIERCE IN THE CAKE JUDGING AT AGRICULTURAL SHOWS, BUT NONE IS TOUGHER THAN SYDNEY'S ROYAL EASTER SHOW WHERE PAMELA CLARK, AUSTRALIAN WOMEN'S WEEKLY TEST KITCHEN DIRECTOR, WAS A RECENT JUDGE. HERE'S HER ACCOUNT OF THIS MOST FAMOUS OF BAKE-OFFS.

"The class I was judging was 'Arts – Cookery: Perishables', an enormously popular category with a huge number of sub-categories and entries. I was ushered into the judging area along with the other three judges and I have never seen anything like it. There were trestles heaving with baked goodies as far as the eye could see.

Feeling the heat The four judges were positioned facing the expectant audience. We each had a microphone so we could relate our innermost thoughts on the entries in front of us. The audience – made up of contestants and interested onlookers – hung on our every word. The place was packed, but you could have heard a pin drop.

Rising temperature Then came the judging. Each judge had runners, who literally ran to us with trays of entries. Any cakes that exhibited obvious visual failings – the sunken, the burnt, the crusty, the rule-breakers – were quickly assessed and eliminated. The cakes that remained were cut and, if they looked questionable in any way, they were eliminated too. In quite a short space of time we were down to twenty or so entries. Then a first, second, third and highly commended had to be selected.

Stand for five hours Sometimes it was easy – the winners were obvious – but this wasn't always the case. I kept going back for another look, another touch, and another taste. The numbered entries were then carefully documented, and then we went onto another batch, and another, and another. We stood there judging for around five hours.

142

the *country* table

Taking the cake I take my hat off to all the people who enter these competitions. The rules are rigid and I guess they have to be. The entrants bake their goodies at some unearthly hour on the morning of the judging and then trek to the venue. The entries are carefully tagged, numbered and covered while they await the judging process but it's a race against time and staling. Despite the care taken, it doesn't take long before the staling process is in full swing. The judges are as fair as they can be given the time constraints and the vast number of entries they have to judge. For judges and entrants alike the whole process is an exercise in logistics and stamina".

Here are Pamela's tips for making an impressive entry at your local show.

Plain scones The scones have to look good first. The browning should be even and they should all be the same height and diameter. Those with a 'waist' get rejected because the dough is too soft. They should be level and smooth on the top, there shouldn't be any sign of excess flour. When you break one open, it should break without crumbling and the texture should be smooth and fine, not aerated or spongy. Then there's the taste: are they too salty? Too sweet? Too buttery? Too soapy (due to too much bicarbonate of soda or raising agent)? And so on.

Sultana scones You look for the same things as in the plain scones, but these scones should be sweeter. The sultanas should be distributed evenly throughout each scone and there should be no burnt ones poking out of the tops. You'll lose points for this.

Butter cakes It's all about how the cake looks first. Has it risen and browned evenly? Are there any white spots (undissolved sugar) dark patches (over-handled scrapings from the bowl) or marks from the wire cooling rack on the top of the cake? Then I look at the texture (the finer the better) and the size of the crumb (the finer the better) and the way the cake has risen. If there's a heavier layer of cake at the bottom then the butter has broken down either by over-creaming or because it was too soft before it was creamed, or the balance of the ingredients was out of kilter. If the cake is tough (caused by too much protein) then once again the balance is out: too much flour, not enough liquid, or too many eggs have been used.

Sponges Like the butter cakes you look at the texture, the crumb structure and check if there's any heaviness at the bottom of the sponge. When it comes to taste, if you feel undissolved sugar in your mouth or taste a certain soapiness it points to too much raising agent. Specks of custard powder can lose points. And you don't want globs of flour on the crust of the sponge. My tip: use a lightly greased (not floured) cake tin.

Winter by the fire

Steaming bowls of soup, fragrant stews and delicious puddings that will put a rose in your cheeks.

SCOTCH BROTH

1kg lamb neck chops
¾ cup (150g) pearl barley
2.25 litres (9 cups) water
1 large brown onion (200g), cut into 1cm pieces
2 medium carrots (240g), cut into 1cm pieces
1 medium leek (350g), sliced thinly
2 cups (160g) finely shredded savoy cabbage
½ cup (60g) frozen peas
2 tablespoons coarsely chopped
fresh flat-leaf parsley

1 Place chops, barley and the water in large saucepan; bring to the boil. Reduce heat; simmer, covered, 1 hour, skimming fat from surface occasionally.
2 Add onion, carrot and leek to pan; simmer, covered, about 30 minutes or until vegetables are tender.
3 Remove chops from soup mixture; when cool enough to handle, remove meat, chop coarsely. Discard bones.
4 Return meat to soup with cabbage and peas; cook, uncovered, about 10 minutes or until cabbage is tender.
5 Just before serving, sprinkle with parsley.

prep and cook time 1 hour 30 minutes
serves 4
nutritional count per serving 24.4g total fat (10.7g saturated fat); 2274kJ (544 cal); 32.8g carbohydrate; 43.2g protein; 10.6g fibre

"I love raiding the vegie garden for whatever is in season, and piling it all into a huge cauldron for a delicious chunky soup."
– Trisha Dixon, Cooma, New South Wales

ABOVE CHUNKY BEEF AND VEGETABLE SOUP
LEFT MINESTRONE

CHUNKY BEEF AND VEGETABLE SOUP

2 tablespoons olive oil
600g gravy beef, trimmed, cut into 2cm pieces
1 medium brown onion (150g), chopped coarsely
1 clove garlic, crushed
1.5 litres (6 cups) water
1 cup (250ml) beef stock
400g can diced tomatoes
2 trimmed celery stalks (200g), cut into 1cm pieces
1 medium carrot (120g), cut into 1cm pieces
2 small potatoes (240g), cut into 1cm pieces
310g can corn kernels, rinsed, drained
½ cup (60g) frozen peas

1 Heat half of the oil in large saucepan; cook beef, in batches, until browned.
2 Heat remaining oil in same pan; cook onion and garlic, stirring, until onion softens. Return beef to pan with the water, stock and undrained tomatoes; bring to the boil. Reduce heat; simmer, covered, 1½ hours.
3 Add celery, carrot and potato to soup; simmer, uncovered, about 20 minutes or until vegetables are tender.
4 Add corn and peas to soup; stir over heat until peas are tender.

prep and cook time 2 hours 20 minutes
serves 4
nutritional count per serving 17g total fat (4.3g saturated fat); 1768kJ (423 cal); 26.7g carbohydrate; 36.9g protein; 7.5g fibre

MINESTRONE

1 cup (200g) dried borlotti beans
1 tablespoon olive oil
1 medium brown onion (150g), chopped coarsely
1 clove garlic, crushed
¼ cup (70g) tomato paste
1.5 litres (6 cups) water
2 cups (500ml) vegetable stock
700g bottled tomato pasta sauce
1 trimmed celery stalk (100g), chopped finely
1 medium carrot (120g), chopped finely
1 medium zucchini (120g), chopped finely
80g green beans, trimmed, chopped finely
¾ cup (135g) macaroni
⅓ cup coarsely chopped fresh basil

1 Place borlotti beans in medium bowl, cover with water; stand overnight, drain. Rinse under cold water; drain.
2 Heat oil in large saucepan; cook onion and garlic, stirring, until onion softens. Add paste; cook, stirring, 2 minutes. Add borlotti beans, the water, stock and pasta sauce; bring to the boil. Reduce heat; simmer, uncovered, about 1 hour or until beans are tender.
3 Add celery to soup; simmer, uncovered, 10 minutes. Add carrot, zucchini and green beans; simmer, uncovered, about 20 minutes or until carrot is tender. Add pasta; simmer until pasta is tender.
4 Serve bowls of soup sprinkled with basil.

prep and cook time 2 hours 30 minutes (plus standing)
serves 6
nutritional count per serving 5.5g total fat (1g saturated fat); 1095kJ (262 cal); 39.9g carbohydrate; 9.4g protein; 6.5g fibre

LAMB SHANK AND VEGETABLE SOUP

4 lamb shanks (1kg)
2 medium carrots (240g), chopped coarsely
2 medium white onions (300g), chopped coarsely
2 cloves garlic, crushed
2 medium potatoes (400g), chopped coarsely
2 trimmed celery stalks (200g), chopped coarsely
400g can chopped tomatoes
1.5 litres (6 cups) beef or chicken stock
½ cup (125ml) tomato paste
2 medium zucchini (240g), chopped coarsely

1 Place shanks, carrot, onion, garlic, potato, celery, undrained tomatoes, stock and paste in large saucepan; bring to the boil. Reduce heat; simmer, covered, 1 hour.
2 Add zucchini to soup, simmer, uncovered, further 30 minutes or until shanks are tender.
3 Remove shanks from soup. When cool enough to handle, remove meat from bones, discard bones. Return meat to soup, stir until heated through.

prep and cook time 2 hours
serves 4
nutritional count per serving 9.2g total fat (3.9g saturated fat); 1513kJ (362 cal); 29.2g carbohydrate; 39.7g protein; 8.5g fibre

ABOVE TOASTED HAM SANDWICH WITH FRIED EGG
LEFT SALMON AND POTATO PATTIES

TOASTED HAM SANDWICH WITH FRIED EGG

8 slices wholemeal bread (360g)

8 slices leg ham (240g)

40g butter

4 eggs

cheese béchamel

20g butter

1 tablespoon plain flour

¾ cup (180ml) milk

½ cup (60g) finely grated cheddar cheese

1 tablespoon finely chopped fresh flat-leaf parsley

1 Make cheese béchamel.
2 Spread béchamel onto bread slices. Top four slices with ham then remaining bread.
3 Melt butter in large frying pan. Add sandwiches; toast, in batches, until browned both sides.
4 Fry eggs in same pan until cooked; place an egg on each sandwich.
cheese béchamel Melt butter in small saucepan, add flour; cook,stirring, until mixture bubbles and thickens. Gradually add milk; cook, stirring, until sauce boils and thickens. Remove from heat; stir in cheese and parsley.

prep and cook time 35 minutes
serves 4
nutritional count per serving 29.2g total fat (15.2g saturated fat); 2328kJ (557 cal); 38.6g carbohydrate; 32.3g protein; 5.8g fibre

SALMON AND POTATO PATTIES

1kg potatoes, peeled

440g can red salmon

1 small brown onion (80g), chopped finely

1 tablespoon finely chopped fresh flat-leaf parsley

1 teaspoon finely grated lemon rind

1 tablespoon lemon juice

½ cup (75g) plain flour

1 egg

2 tablespoons milk

½ cup (50g) packaged breadcrumbs

½ cup (35g) stale breadcrumbs

vegetable oil, for deep-frying

1 Boil, steam or microwave potatoes until tender; drain. Mash potato in large bowl.
2 Drain salmon; discard any skin and bones. Add salmon to potato with onion, parsley, rind and juice; mix well. Cover; refrigerate 30 minutes.
3 Using floured hands, shape salmon mixture into eight patties. Toss patties in flour; shake away excess. Dip patties, one at a time, in combined egg and milk, then in combined breadcrumbs.
4 Heat oil in wok; deep-fry patties, in batches, until browned lightly. Drain on absorbent paper.

prep and cook time 40 minutes (plus refrigeration)
makes 8
nutritional count per patty 16.7g total fat (3.1g saturated fat); 1396kJ (334 cal); 28.6g carbohydrate; 15.9g protein; 2.7g fibre

STEAK AND KIDNEY PIE

300g beef ox kidneys

1.5g beef chuck steak, chopped coarsely

2 medium brown onions (300g), sliced thinly

1 cup (250ml) beef stock

1 tablespoon soy sauce

¼ cup (35g) plain flour

½ cup (125ml) water

2 sheets ready-rolled puff pastry

1 egg, beaten lightly

1 Remove fat from kidneys; chop kidneys finely. Place kidneys, steak, onion, stock and sauce in large saucepan; simmer, covered, about 1 hour or until steak is tender.
2 Preheat oven to 200°C/180°C fan-forced.
3 Stir blended flour and water into beef mixture; stir until mixture boils and thickens. Transfer to 1.5-litre (6-cup) ovenproof dish.
4 Cut pastry into 6cm rounds. Overlap rounds on beef mixture; brush with egg. Bake pies about 15 minutes or until browned.

prep and cook time 1 hour 50 minutes
serves 6
nutritional count per serving 25.8g total fat (12.2g saturated fat); 2546kJ (609 cal); 27.2g carbohydrate; 65.9g protein; 1.6g fibre

> "So many of my favourite winter foods are comforting and nostalgic and transport me back to my childhood."
> – Jean Kelly
> Dubbo, New South Wales

ABOVE BEEF STEW WITH PARSLEY DUMPLINGS
LEFT SHEPHERD'S PIE

BEEF STEW WITH PARSLEY DUMPLINGS

1kg beef chuck steak, cut into 5cm pieces

2 tablespoons plain flour

2 tablespoons olive oil

20g butter

2 medium brown onions (300g), chopped coarsely

2 cloves garlic, crushed

2 medium carrots (240g), chopped coarsely

1 cup (250ml) dry red wine

2 tablespoons tomato paste

2 cups (500ml) beef stock

4 sprigs fresh thyme

parsley dumplings

1 cup (150g) self-raising flour

50g butter

1 egg, beaten lightly

¼ cup (20g) coarsely grated parmesan cheese

¼ cup finely chopped fresh flat-leaf parsley

⅓ cup (50g) drained sun-dried tomatoes, chopped

¼ cup (60ml) milk

1 Preheat oven to 180°C/160°C fan-forced.
2 Coat beef in flour; shake off excess. Heat oil in large flameproof dish; cook beef, in batches, until browned.
3 Melt butter in same dish; cook onion, garlic and carrot, stirring, until vegetables soften. Add wine; cook, stirring, until liquid reduces to ¼ cup. Return beef with paste, stock and thyme; bring to the boil. Cover; cook in oven 1¾ hours.
4 Meanwhile, make parsley dumpling mixture.
5 Remove dish from oven. Drop level tablespoons of dumpling mixture, about 2cm apart, onto top of stew. Cook, uncovered, about 20 minutes or until dumplings are browned lightly and cooked through.
parsley dumplings Place flour in medium bowl; rub in butter. Stir in egg, cheese, parsley, tomato and enough milk to make a soft, sticky dough.

prep and cook time 2 hours 30 minutes *serves* 4
nutritional count per serving 39.7g total fat (17.4g saturated fat); 3457kJ (827 cal); 43g carbohydrate; 63.9g protein; 6.7g fibre

SHEPHERD'S PIE

30g butter

1 medium brown onion (150g), chopped finely

1 medium carrot (120g), chopped finely

½ teaspoon dried mixed herbs

4 cups (750g) chopped cooked lamb

¼ cup (70g) tomato paste

¼ cup (60ml) tomato sauce

2 tablespoons worcestershire sauce

2 cups (500ml) beef stock

2 tablespoons plain flour

⅓ cup (80ml) water

potato topping

5 medium potatoes (1kg), chopped

60g butter, chopped

¼ cup (60ml) milk

1 Preheat oven to 200°C/180°C fan-forced. Oil shallow 2.5-litre (10-cup) ovenproof dish.
2 Make potato topping.
3 Heat butter in large saucepan; cook onion and carrot, stirring, until tender. Add mixed herbs and lamb; cook, stirring, 2 minutes. Stir in paste, sauces and stock, then blended flour and water; stir over heat until mixture boils and thickens. Pour mixture into dish.
4 Place heaped tablespoons of potato topping on lamb mixture. Bake about 20 minutes or until browned lightly and heated through.
potato topping Boil, steam or microwave potatoes until tender; drain. Mash with butter and milk until smooth.

prep and cook time 1 hour
serves 4
nutritional count per serving 36.2g total fat (20.2g saturated fat); 2976kJ (712 cal); 44.7g carbohydrate; 48.8g protein; 6.6g fibre

"Winter is about sharing the luxury of a slow cooked stew and peppery shiraz in front of a blazing fire with warm-hearted friends."
– Hilary Burden, Karoola, Tasmania

TUNA MORNAY

30g butter

1 medium brown onion (150g), chopped finely

1 trimmed celery stalk (100g), chopped finely

1 tablespoon plain flour

¾ cup (180ml) milk

½ cup (125ml) cream

⅓ cup (40g) grated cheddar cheese

130g can corn kernels, drained

2 x 185g can tuna, drained

1 cup (70g) stale breadcrumbs

¼ cup (30g) grated cheddar cheese, extra

1 Preheat oven to 180°C/160°C fan-forced.
2 Melt butter in medium saucepan; cook onion and celery, stirring, until onion is soft. Add flour; cook, stirring, 1 minute. Gradually stir in combined milk and cream; cook, stirring, until mixture boils and thickens. Remove pan from heat, add cheese, corn and tuna; stir until cheese is melted.
3 Spoon mornay mixture into four 1½-cup (375ml) ovenproof dishes. Sprinkle with combined breadcrumbs and extra cheese.
4 Bake tuna mornay about 15 minutes or until heated through.

prep and cook time 10 minutes
serves 4
nutritional count per serving 30.2g total fat (18.8g saturated fat); 2031kJ (486 cal); 23.4g carbohydrate; 29.3g protein; 2.5g fibre

161

winter by the *fire*

CURRIED SAUSAGES

800g thick beef sausages

20g butter

1 medium brown onion (150g), chopped coarsely

1 tablespoon curry powder

2 teaspoons plain flour

2 large carrots (360g), chopped coarsely

2 trimmed celery stalks (200g), chopped coarsely

500g baby new potatoes, halved

2 cups (500ml) beef stock

1 cup loosely packed fresh flat-leaf parsley leaves

1 Cook sausages, in batches, in heated deep large frying pan until cooked through. Cut each sausage into thirds.
2 Melt butter in same cleaned pan; cook onion, stirring, until soft. Add curry powder and flour; cook, stirring, 2 minutes.
3 Add vegetables and stock; bring to the boil. Reduce heat; simmer, covered, about 15 minutes or until vegetables are tender. Add sausages; simmer, uncovered, until sauce thickens slightly. Stir in parsley.

prep and cook time 55 minutes
serves 4
nutritional count per serving 55.8g total fat (27.3g saturated fat); 3177kJ (760 cal); 29.8g carbohydrate; 30.1g protein; 12.8g fibre

RISSOLE, BACON AND TOMATO CASSEROLE

600g beef mince

1 small brown onion (80g), chopped finely

1 egg

½ cup (100g) white long-grain rice

¼ cup (15g) stale breadcrumbs

2 teaspoons worcestershire sauce

4 bacon rashers (280g), chopped finely

400g can diced tomatoes

½ cup (125ml) beef stock

2 tablespoon tomato paste

½ cup coarsely chopped fresh basil

1 Preheat oven to 200°C/180°C fan-forced.
2 Combine mince, onion, egg, rice, breadcrumbs and sauce in large bowl. Shape mixture into 12 rissoles; place into deep 2-litre (8-cup) ovenproof dish.
3 Sprinkle bacon over rissoles; pour over combined tomatoes, stock and paste.
4 Bake casserole, covered, 1 hour or until rissoles are cooked through and rice is tender. Stir in basil before serving.

prep and cook time 1 hour 15 minutes
serves 4
nutritional count per serving 27.4g total fat (11g saturated fat); 2353kJ (563 cal); 28.8g carbohydrate; 49.1g protein; 2.4g fibre

TIP CURRY POWDER IS A BLEND OF GROUND SPICES, WHICH USUALLY INCLUDE CORIANDER, DRIED CHILLI, CUMIN, CINNAMON, FENNEL, FENUGREEK, MACE, CARDAMOM AND TURMERIC. AVAILABLE MILD OR HOT, USE ACCORDING TO YOUR TASTE PREFERENCE.

TOP, CENTRE CURRIED SAUSAGES
ABOVE RISSOLE, BACON AND TOMATO CASSEROLE

winter by the *fire*

CURRIED CHICKEN PIES

1.6kg chicken

90g butter

1 small leek (200g), chopped finely

1 medium white onion (150g), chopped finely

1 medium red capsicum (200g), chopped finely

2 trimmed celery stalks (200g), chopped finely

3 teaspoons curry powder

¼ teaspoon chilli powder

¼ cup (35g) plain flour

⅓ cup (80g) sour cream

½ cup finely chopped fresh flat-leaf parsley

2 sheets ready-rolled puff pastry

1 egg, beaten lightly

1 Place chicken in large saucepan, add enough water to just cover chicken; bring to the boil. Reduce heat; simmer, uncovered, 1 hour. Remove pan from heat; when cool enough to handle, remove chicken from stock. Reserve 1¾ cups (430ml) of the stock for this recipe.
2 Preheat oven to 200°C/180°C fan-forced.
3 Remove skin and bones from chicken; chop chicken flesh roughly.
4 Heat butter in large frying pan, add leek, onion, capsicum and celery; cook, stirring, until vegetables are soft.
5 Add curry powder and chilli powder; cook, stirring, until fragrant. Stir in flour. Add reserved stock, stir over heat until mixture boils and thickens; reduce heat, simmer 1 minute, remove from heat. Stir in sour cream, chicken and parsley. Spoon mixture into six 1¼-cup (310ml) ovenproof dishes.
6 Cut pastry into six rounds large enough to cover top of each dish. Lightly brush pastry with egg. Place pies on oven tray.
7 Bake pies 10 minutes. Reduce oven to 180°C/160°C fan-forced; bake further 15 minutes or until pastry is golden brown.

prep and cook time 2 hours 30 minutes (plus standing)
serves 6
nutritional count per serving 52.8g total fat (25.4g saturated fat); 3001kJ (718 cal); 28.5g carbohydrate; 33.3g protein; 3g fibre

THE BEAUTY OF THESE INDIVIDUAL PIES IS THAT YOU CAN FREEZE THEM AND HAVE THEM AT THE READY FOR THE NEXT TIME YOU NEED A WARM-YOU-UP DINNER FOR ONE OR MORE.

"We'll often rug up and go for a walk while the fruit crumble bubbles all caramel in the oven."
– Hilary Burden,
Karoola, Tasmania

ABOVE COLLEGE PUDDING
LEFT APPLE CRUMBLE

COLLEGE PUDDING

⅓ cup (110g) raspberry jam
1 egg
½ cup (110g) caster sugar
1 cup (150g) self-raising flour
½ cup (125ml) milk
25g butter, melted
1 tablespoon boiling water
1 teaspoon vanilla extract

1 Grease four 1-cup (250ml) metal moulds; divide jam among moulds.
2 Beat egg and sugar in small bowl with electric mixer until thick and creamy. Fold in sifted flour and milk, in two batches; fold in combined butter, the water and extract.
3 Spoon pudding mixture over jam. Cover each mould with pleated baking paper and foil (to allow puddings to expand as they cook); secure with kitchen string.
4 Place puddings in large saucepan with enough boiling water to come halfway up sides of moulds. Cover pan with tight-fitting lid; boil 25 minutes, replenishing water as necessary to maintain level. Stand in moulds 5 minutes; turn onto serving plates. Serve puddings with cream, if desired.

prep and cook time 35 minutes
serves 4
nutritional count per serving 8.1g total fat (4.7g saturated fat); 1676kJ (401 cal); 73.7g carbohydrate; 6.5g protein; 1.7g fibre

APPLE CRUMBLE

5 large apples (1kg)
¼ cup (55g) caster sugar
¼ cup (60ml) water
crumble
½ cup (75g) self-raising flour
¼ cup (35g) plain flour
½ cup (110g) firmly packed brown sugar
100g cold butter, chopped
1 teaspoon ground cinnamon

1 Preheat oven to 180°C/160°C fan-forced. Grease deep 1.5-litre (6-cup) baking dish.
2 Peel, core and quarter apples. Cook apples, sugar and the water in large saucepan over low heat, covered, about 10 minutes. Drain; discard liquid.
3 Meanwhile, make crumble.
4 Place apples in dish; sprinkle with crumble. Bake about 25 minutes.
crumble Blend or process ingredients until combined.

prep and cook time 45 minutes
serves 4
nutritional count per serving 21g total fat (13.6g saturated fat); 2240kJ (536 cal); 80.7g carbohydrate; 3.6g protein; 4.5g fibre

STICKY DATE PUDDING WITH BUTTERSCOTCH SAUCE

1¼ cups (200g) seeded dried dates
1¼ cups (310ml) boiling water
1 teaspoon bicarbonate of soda
50g butter, chopped
½ cup (100g) firmly packed brown sugar
2 eggs, beaten lightly
1 cup (150g) self-raising flour

butterscotch sauce
¾ cup (150g) firmly packed brown sugar
300ml cream
80g butter

1 Preheat oven to 180°C/160°C fan-forced. Grease deep 20cm-round cake pan; line base and side with baking paper.
2 Combine dates and the water in medium heatproof bowl. Stir in soda; stand 5 minutes.
3 Blend or process date mixture with butter and sugar until pureed. Add eggs and flour; blend or process until just combined. Pour mixture into pan.
4 Bake cake about 1 hour. Stand in pan 10 minutes; turn onto serving plate
5 Meanwhile, make butterscotch sauce.
6 Serve cake warm with butterscotch sauce.
butterscotch sauce Stir ingredients in medium saucepan over low heat until smooth.

prep and cook time 1 hour 10 minutes (plus standing)
serves 6
nutritional count per serving 41.5g total fat (26.6g saturated fat); 3068kJ (734 cal); 82g carbohydrate; 6.5g protein; 4.2g fibre

"Winter for me means crackling fires with a mulled wine in hand, good conversation with family and friends, a pile of good books and music wafting through the house."
— Trisha Dixon, Cooma, New South Wales

GOLDEN SYRUP DUMPLINGS

1¼ cups (185g) self-raising flour

30g butter

⅓ cup (115g) golden syrup

⅓ cup (80ml) milk

sauce

30g butter

¾ cup (165g) firmly packed brown sugar

½ cup (175g) golden syrup

1⅔ cups (410ml) water

1 Sift flour into medium bowl; rub in butter. Gradually stir in golden syrup and milk.
2 Make sauce.
3 Drop rounded tablespoonfuls of mixture into simmering sauce; simmer, covered, about 20 minutes. Serve dumplings with sauce.
sauce Stir ingredients in medium saucepan over heat, without boiling, until sugar dissolves. Bring to the boil, without stirring. Reduce heat; simmer, uncovered, 5 minutes.

prep and cook time 30 minutes
serves 4
nutritional count per serving 13.6g total fat (8.7g saturated fat); 2788kJ (667 cal); 128g carbohydrate; 5.6g protein; 1.8g fibre

THESE DUMPLINGS ARE MADE FROM A SCONE-TYPE DOUGH. COOKING THEM IN THE SAUCE INFUSES THEM WITH THE SWEET FLAVOUR. YOU'LL NEED TO USE A SAUCEPAN LARGE ENOUGH TO ALLOW THE DUMPLINGS TO EXPAND IN THE SIMMERING SAUCE. IF THE DUMPLINGS DON'T EXPAND THEY WON'T COOK THROUGH. IF THE PAN IS TOO LARGE, TOO MUCH OF THE SAUCE WILL EVAPORATE BEFORE THE DUMPLINGS ARE ADDED.

BREAD AND BUTTER PUDDING

6 slices white bread (270g)

40g butter, softened

½ cup (80g) sultanas

¼ teaspoon ground nutmeg

custard

1½ cups (375ml) milk

2 cups (500ml) cream

⅓ cup (75g) caster sugar

½ teaspoon vanilla extract

4 eggs

1 Preheat oven to 160°C/140°C fan-forced. Grease shallow 2-litre (8-cup) ovenproof dish.
2 Make custard.
3 Trim crusts from bread. Spread each slice with butter; cut into four triangles. Layer bread, overlapping, in dish; sprinkle with sultanas. Pour custard over bread; sprinkle with nutmeg.
4 Place dish in large baking dish; add enough boiling water to come halfway up sides of dish.
5 Bake pudding about 45 minutes or until set. Remove pudding from baking dish; stand 5 minutes before serving.
custard Bring milk, cream, sugar and extract in medium saucepan to the boil. Whisk eggs in large bowl; whisking constantly, gradually add hot milk mixture to egg mixture.

prep and cook time 1 hour 10 minutes
serves 6
nutritional count per serving 48.6g total fat (30.4g saturated fat); 2859kJ (684 cal); 49.3g carbohydrate; 12.4g protein; 1.8g fibre

ABOVE CHOCOLATE SELF-SAUCING PUDDING
RIGHT BAKED CUSTARD

CHOCOLATE SELF-SAUCING PUDDING

60g butter
½ cup (125ml) milk
½ teaspoon vanilla extract
¾ cup (165g) caster sugar
1 cup (150g) self-raising flour
1 tablespoon cocoa powder
¾ cup (165g) firmly packed brown sugar
1 tablespoon cocoa powder, extra
2 cups (500ml) boiling water

1 Preheat oven to 180°C/160°C fan-forced. Grease 1.5-litre (6-cup) ovenproof dish.
2 Melt butter with milk in medium saucepan. Remove from heat; stir in extract and caster sugar then sifted flour and cocoa. Spread mixture into dish.
3 Sift brown sugar and extra cocoa over mixture; gently pour boiling water over mixture.
4 Bake pudding about 40 minutes or until centre is firm. Stand 5 minutes before serving.

prep and cook time 1 hour
serves 6
nutritional count per serving 9.7g total fat (6.2g saturated fat); 1676kJ (401 cal); 73.4g carbohydrate; 3.8g protein; 1.1g fibre

BAKED CUSTARD

6 eggs
1 teaspoon vanilla extract
⅓ cup (75g) caster sugar
1 litre (4 cups) hot milk
¼ teaspoon ground nutmeg

1 Preheat oven to 160°C/140°C fan-forced. Grease shallow 1.5-litre (6-cup) ovenproof dish.
2 Whisk eggs, extract and sugar in large bowl; gradually whisk in hot milk. Pour custard mixture into dish; sprinkle with nutmeg.
3 Place dish in larger baking dish; add enough boiling water to baking dish to come halfway up sides of dish.
4 Bake custard, uncovered, about 45 minutes. Remove custard from baking dish; stand 5 minutes before serving.

prep and cook time 50 minutes
serves 6
nutritional count per serving 11.8g total fat (5.9g saturated fat); 995kJ (238 cal); 20.7g carbohydrate; 12.3g protein; 0g fibre

the jam pan

Home-made jams, preserves and relishes have been a mainstay of country kitchens for generations.

PEACH AND PASSIONFRUIT JAM

You will need about 9 passionfruit for this recipe.

4 large peaches (800g)
½ cup (125ml) lemon juice
½ cup (125ml) water
2½ cups (550g) sugar, approximately
¾ cup (180ml) passionfruit pulp
2 tablespoons peach liqueur

1 Peel and halve peaches, discard stones; chop finely. Place peaches, juice and water in large saucepan; bring to the boil. Reduce heat; simmer, covered, 20 minutes or until peaches are soft.
2 Measure fruit mixture; allow ¾ cup (165g) sugar for each cup of fruit mixture.
3 Return fruit mixture and sugar to pan; stir over heat, without boiling, until sugar dissolves. Boil, uncovered, without stirring, 15 minutes or until jam gels when tested. Stir in passionfruit and liqueur.
4 Pour into hot sterilised jars; seal immediately.

prep and cook time 1 hour (plus cooling)
makes 3 cups
nutritional count per tablespoon 0g total fat (0g saturated fat); 314kJ (75 cal); 17.3g carbohydrate; 0.3g protein; 0.9g fibre

GRAPEFRUIT AND GINGER MARMALADE

2 medium lemons (280g)
2 medium grapefruit (850g)
6cm piece fresh ginger (30g)
2.5 litres (10 cups) water
1 teaspoon tartaric acid
1.75kg (8 cups) white sugar
1 cup (180g) finely chopped glacé ginger

1 Peel lemons; chop rind coarsely. Chop flesh coarsely; reserve seeds and juice. Peel grapefruit, chop rind into fine strips; reserve. Chop flesh coarsely; reserve seeds and juice.
2 Combine lemon and grapefruit flesh with reserved juice in large saucepan. Tie reserved seeds, lemon rind and fresh peeled ginger in piece of muslin, add to pan. Add grapefruit rind with the water and acid; bring to the boil. Boil, uncovered, about 1½ hours or until rind is soft and mixture has reduced by half. Discard muslin bag.
3 Add sugar; stir, without boiling, until sugar dissolves. Boil, uncovered, without stirring, 15 minutes or until marmalade gels. Add glacé ginger; stand 10 minutes.
4 Pour into hot sterilised jars; seal immediately.

prep and cook time 2 hours 25 minutes (plus cooling)
makes 2 litres (8 cups)
nutritional count per tablespoon 0g total fat (0g saturated); 343kJ (82 cal); 20.1g carbohydrate; 0.1g protein; 0.1g fibre

"In days gone by, preserving was a way of ensuring the family had summer fruit all year round. Those jars of beautifully bottled fruit lined up on the kitchen shelves were a joy to behold."
— Pamela Clark

LEFT PEACH AND PASSIONFRUIT JAM
RIGHT GRAPEFUIT AND GINGER MARMALADE

"There's a therapeutic element to preserving. It's a creative and sustainable way to treat your produce."
– Virginia Imhoff, Kingston, Victoria

ABOVE DARK PLUM JAM
LEFT SPICED FIG AND APPLE JAM

DARK PLUM JAM

28 medium blood plums (2kg)

1 litre (4 cups) water

⅓ cup (80ml) lemon juice

1.3kg (6 cups) white sugar

1 Cut plums into quarters; discard stones. Place plums and the water in large saucepan; bring to the boil. Reduce heat; simmer, covered, 1 hour.
2 Add juice and sugar, stir over heat, without boiling, until sugar dissolves. Boil, uncovered, without stirring, 20 minutes or until jam gels when tested.
3 Pour into hot sterilised jars; seal immediately.

prep and cook time 1 hour 45 minutes (plus cooling)
makes 2 litres (8 cups)
nutritional count per tablespoon 0g total fat (0g saturated); 255kJ (61 cal); 14.7g carbohydrate; 0.1g protein; 0.4g fibre

SPICED FIG APPLE JAM

Finely grate the rind from the oranges before juicing them.

2 large granny smith apples (500g), peeled, chopped finely

2 cups (500ml) water

16 medium fresh figs (1 kg), chopped coarsely

½ cup (125ml) orange juice

1.1kg (5 cups) caster sugar, approximately

2 tablespoons finely grated orange rind

1 teaspoon ground cinnamon

pinch ground cloves

1 Bring apple and the water in large saucepan to the boil. Reduce heat; simmer, covered, about 20 minutes or until apples are soft. Add figs and juice; simmer, covered, 10 minutes.
2 Measure fruit mixture; allow ¾ cup (165g) sugar for each cup of mixture.
3 Return fruit mixture and sugar to pan with remaining ingredients; stir over heat, without boiling, until sugar dissolves. Boil, uncovered, 45 minutes or until jam gels when tested.
4 Pour into hot sterilised jars; seal immediately.

prep and cook time 1 hour 30 minutes (plus cooling)
makes 2 litres (8 cups)
nutritional count per tablespoon 0g total fat (0g saturated fat); 226kJ (54 cal); 12.9g carbohydrate; 0.2g protein; 0.3g fibre

STRAWBERRY CONSERVE

1.5kg strawberries, hulled

1.1kg (5 cups) white sugar

1 cup (250ml) lemon juice

1 Gently heat berries in large saucepan, covered, for 5 minutes to extract juice from berries. Transfer berries with slotted spoon to large bowl; reserve.
2 Add sugar and lemon juice to pan, stir over heat, without boiling, until sugar dissolves; bring to the boil. Boil, uncovered, without stirring, 20 minutes. Add reserved berries to pan; simmer, uncovered, without stirring, 25 minutes or until jam gels when tested.
3 Pour jam into hot sterilised jars; seal immediately.

prep and cook time 1 hour 10 minutes (plus cooling)
makes 1.5 litres (6 cups)
nutritional count per tablespoon 0g total fat (0g saturated); 280kJ (67 cal); 15.9g carbohydrate; 0.4g protein; 0.5g fibre

APPLE AND APRICOT JAM

18 medium apricots (750g)

5 large apples (1kg), peeled, chopped

3 cups (750ml) water

1kg (4 cups) sugar, approximately

1 Halve apricots; discard stones. Place apricots, apples and the water in large saucepan; bring to the boil. Reduce heat; simmer, covered, 30 minutes.
2 Measure fruit mixture, allow ¾ cup (165g) sugar to each cup of fruit mixture. Return fruit mixture and sugar to pan; stir over heat, without boiling, until sugar is dissolved. Boil, uncovered, without stirring, about 30 minutes or until jam jells when tested.
3 Pour into hot sterilised jars; seal immediately.

prep and cook time 1 hour 30 minutes (plus cooling)
makes 1.5 litres (6 cups)
nutritional count per tablespoon 0g total fat (0g saturated fat); 276kJ (66 cal); 15.9g carbohydrate; 0.1g protein; 0.4g fibre

CITRUS MARMALADE

Lime rind will take the longest time to cook, so it's the one to check; it must be very soft.

4 large oranges (1.2kg)

3 medium lemons (420g)

4 large limes (400g)

1.25 litres (5 cups) water

1.6kg (7 cups) white sugar, approximately

1 Peel all fruit thinly; cut rind into thin strips. Remove pith from all fruit; reserve half, discard remaining pith. Chop flesh coarsely, reserve seeds.
2 Combine flesh and rind in large bowl with the water. Tie reserved pith and seeds in muslin; add to bowl. Stand at room temperature overnight.
3 Place fruit mixture and muslin bag in large saucepan; bring to the boil. Reduce heat; simmer, covered, 25 minutes or until rind is soft. Discard bag.
4 Measure fruit mixture; allow 1 cup (220g) sugar for each cup of mixture.
5 Return mixture and sugar to pan; stir over heat, without boiling, until sugar dissolves. Boil, uncovered, about 40 minutes or until marmalade gels when tested.
6 Pour into hot sterilised jars; seal immediately.

prep and cook time 1 hour 50 minutes (plus standing and cooling)
makes 1.75 litres (7 cups)
nutritional count per tablespoon 0g total fat (0g saturated fat); 326kJ (78 cal); 18.8g carbohydrate; 0.2g protein; 0.5g fibre

TIP JAM INGREDIENTS ARE ABUNDANT IN THE SUMMER MONTHS AND PRESERVING THEM IS A DELICIOUS WAY TO EXTEND THE LIFE OF YOUR FAVOURITE FRUITS. HOME-MADE JAMS ALSO MAKE GREAT GIFTS FOR FRIENDS AND FAMILY.

TOP, CENTRE STRAWBERRY CONSERVE
ABOVE, LEFT APPLE AND APRICOT JAM
LEFT CITRUS MARMALADE

185

the *jam* pan

186

the *country* table

"What better way to celebrate the summer harvest than with freshly made scones spread with lashings of home-made berry jam."

– Pamela Clark

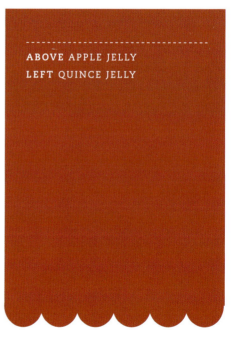

ABOVE APPLE JELLY
LEFT QUINCE JELLY

188

the *country* table

APPLE JELLY

5 medium sour green apples (750g),
  chopped coarsely
1½ litres (6 cups) water
4 cups (880g) white sugar, approximately

1 Place apples (seeds, skin, cores and all) and the water in large saucepan; bring to the boil. Simmer, covered, 1 hour. Strain mixture through fine cloth; discard pulp.
2 Measure apple liquid; allow 1 cup (220g) of sugar for each cup of liquid.
3 Place apple liquid and sugar in large saucepan; stir over heat, without boiling, until sugar dissolves. Bring to the boil; boil, uncovered, 15 minutes or until jelly sets.
4 Pour into hot sterilised jars; seal immediately.

prep and cook time 1 hour 25 minutes (plus cooling)
makes 3 cups
nutritional count per tablespoon 0g total fat (0g saturated); 447kJ (107 cal); 26.2g carbohydrate; 0.1g protein; 0.3g fibre

QUINCE JELLY

6 large quinces (2kg)
1.75 litres (7 cups) water
1.1kg (5 cups) white sugar, approximately
½ cup (125ml) lemon juice, strained

1 Chop unpeeled, uncored quinces coarsely. Place quince and the water in large saucepan; bring to the boil. Reduce heat; simmer, covered, about 1 hour or until quince is soft.
2 Strain quince mixture through fine cloth; stand overnight. Allow liquid to drip through cloth slowly, do not squeeze cloth; discard pulp.
3 Measure quince liquid; allow 1 cup (220g) of sugar for each cup of quince liquid.
4 Place quince liquid and sugar in large saucepan; stir over heat, without boiling, until sugar dissolves. Stir in juice, bring to the boil; boil, uncovered, without stirring, about 25 minutes or until jelly sets when tested.
5 Pour into hot sterilised jars; seal immediately.

prep and cook time 1 hour 35 minutes
(plus standing and cooling)
makes 1.25 litres (5 cups)
nutritional count per tablespoon 0g total fat (0g saturated fat); 343kJ (82 cal); 20.9g carbohydrate; 0.1g protein; 1.7g fibre

SPICY TOMATO CHUTNEY

10 medium ripe tomatoes (1.5kg), peeled, chopped coarsely
2 large apples (400g), peeled, chopped coarsely
2 medium brown onions (300g), chopped coarsely
1 cup (220g) firmly packed brown sugar
1½ cups (375ml) brown vinegar
¼ teaspoon chilli powder
½ teaspoon dry mustard
¾ cup (120g) sultanas
1 clove garlic, crushed
2 teaspoons curry powder
2 teaspoons ground allspice

1 Stir ingredients in large saucepan over heat, without boiling, until sugar dissolves; bring to the boil. Reduce heat; simmer, uncovered, stirring occasionally, about 1 hour or until mixture is thick.
2 Pour into hot sterilised jars; seal immediately.

prep and cook time 1 hour 30 minutes (plus cooling)
makes 1.5 litres (6 cups)
nutritional count per tablespoon 0g total fat (0g saturated); 100kJ (24 cal); 5.3g carbohydrate; 0.3g protein; 0.5g fibre

SPICY MUSTARD PICKLES

¼ medium cauliflower (400g), chopped coarsely
250g green beans, trimmed, chopped coarsely
3 medium brown onions (450g), sliced thickly
1 medium red capsicum (200g), sliced thickly
¼ cup (70g) coarse cooking salt
2 teaspoons dry mustard
2 tablespoons wholegrain mustard
3 teaspoons curry powder
¼ teaspoon ground turmeric
2 cups (500ml) white vinegar
1 cup (220g) firmly packed brown sugar
2 tablespoons plain flour

1 Combine vegetables and salt in large bowl. Cover; stand overnight.
2 Rinse vegetables; drain. Stir vegetables, mustards, curry powder, turmeric, 1¾ cups of the vinegar and sugar in large saucepan over heat, without boiling, until sugar dissolves; bring to the boil. Simmer, uncovered, about 10 minutes or until vegetables are just tender.
3 Stir in blended flour and remaining vinegar; stir over heat until mixture boils and thickens. Pour into hot sterilised jars; seal.

prep and cook time 50 minutes (plus standing and cooling)
makes 4 cups
nutritional count per tablespoon 0.1g total fat (0g saturated); 113kJ (27 cal); 5.7g carbohydrate; 0.6g protein; 0.5g fibre

"My mother used homegrown zucchini and tomatoes in her summer relishes – a great accompaniment to a ploughman's lunch on a hot day."
– Rachael Flynn, Mudgee, NSW

RIGHT SPICY TOMATO CHUTNEY
BELOW, RIGHT SPICY MUSTARD PICKLES

"Country cooking is associated with conviviality. Whether it's a romantic notion or not, it's a notion that keeps coming back, so it must have some basis of truth. Maybe it relates back to another time when city folk would go and visit their country family and they would be served generous roast dinners."

– Stefano di Pieri

GLOSSARY

almond meal – also known as ground almonds; nuts are ground to a coarse flour texture for use in baking or as a thickening agent.

allspice – also known as pimento or jamaican pepper. Available whole (a dark-brown berry the size of a pea) or ground, and used in both sweet and savoury dishes.

bake blind – a term to describe baking a pie shell or pastry case before filling is added. When a filling doesn't need to be baked or is very wet, you might need to 'blind-bake' the pastry shell. To bake blind, line the pastry with baking paper then fill with dried beans, uncooked rice or 'baking beans' (these are also called pie weights). Bake according to the directions then cool before adding the filling.

baking paper – also known as parchment, silicon paper or non-stick baking paper; used to line pans before cooking and baking.

baste – to moisten meat while cooking: for example, with a coating of olive oil or butter.

bicarbonate of soda – also known as baking soda; a mild alkali used as a leavening agent in baking.

borlotti beans – also known as roman beans or pink beans, can be eaten fresh or dried.

BEEF
chuck steak – an inexpensive cut of beef from the neck and shoulder area; good minced and slow-cooked.
corned beef – also known as corned silverside; contains little fat, cut from the upper leg and cured.
gravy beef – boneless stewing beef cut from shin. Slow-cooked, it imbues stocks, soups and casseroles with a gelatine richness. Cut crossways, with bone in, is osso buco.
ox kidneys – originally from the ox but these days more likely to be from any beef cattle.
silverside – also known as topside roast; this is the actual cut used for making corned beef.
standing rib roast – a cut of beef, also known as a scotch fillet. Cut from the muscle running behind the shoulder along the spine.

CABBAGE
savoy – a flavourful, crinkled leaf cabbage which is one of the best for cooking.

CHEESE
cheddar – the most common cow-milk tasty cheese; should be aged, hard and have a pronounced bite.
cottage – fresh, white, unripened curd cheese with a lumpy consistency and mild flavour.

chervil – also known as cicily; mildly fennel-flavoured member of the parsley family with curly dark-green leaves. Available fresh and dried but is best used fresh.

chipolata sausages – a small pork sausage that is seasoned with spices such as chives, cloves, coriander and thyme.

cocoa powder – also known as unsweetened cocoa; cocoa beans that have been fermented, roasted, shelled, ground into powder then cleared of most of the fat content.

COCONUT
desiccated – concentrated, dried, unsweetened and finely shredded coconut flesh.
shredded – unsweetened thin strips of dried coconut flesh.
flaked – dried, flaked coconut flesh.

cornflour – also known as cornstarch. Available made from corn or wheat (wheaten cornflour, gluten-free, gives a lighter texture in cakes); used as a thickening agent in cooking.

cranberries – a firm, sour, edible, red berry, available, dried, in packets from most supermarkets.

cream of tartar – the acid ingredient in baking powder.

custard powder – instant mixture used to make pouring custard.

GLOSSARY

flat-leaf parsley – also known as continental or Italian parsley. Is stronger in flavour and darker in colour than curley parsley.

FLOUR
plain – also known as all-purpose.
rice – very fine, almost powdery, gluten-free flour made from ground white rice.
self raising – all-purpose plain or wholemeal flour with baking powder and salt added.

green onions – also known as scallion or (incorrectly) shallot; an immature onion picked before the bulb has formed, having a long, bright-green edible stalk.

juniper berries – these berries have a bittersweet taste. They're used widely in Northern Europe and Scandinavia in marinades, roast pork, and sauerkraut.

kumara – the polynesian name of an orange-fleshed sweet potato often confused with yam.

LAMB
shanks – meat from the forequarter leg.
french-trimmed – a forequarter leg with the gristle and narrow end of the bone removed and remaining meat trimmed.

MILK – we use full-cream homogenised milk unless otherwise specified.
buttermilk – originally the term given to the slightly sour liquid left after butter was churned from cream, buttermilk today is commercially made similarly to yogurt. In spite of its name, buttermilk is actually low in fat.
evaporated – unsweetened canned milk from which water has been evaporated.
sweetened condensed – milk with more than half the water content removed and sugar added to the remaining milk.

MUSHROOMS
button – small, white mushrooms with a mild flavour. We use button mushrooms unless otherwise unspecified.

pepitas – the pale green kernels of dried pumpkin seeds; they can be bought plain or salted.

pearl barley – a nutritious grain used in soups and stews. Pearl barley has had the husk removed then been hulled and polished so only the "pearl" of the original grain remains.

polenta – also known as cornmeal; a flour-like cereal made of dried corn (maize).

POTATOES
baby new – also known as chats; good unpeeled, steamed, eaten hot or cold in salads.

RICE
Long grain – elongated grains that remain separate when cooked; this is the most popular steaming rice in Asia.

quince – yellow-skinned fruit with hard texture and astringent, tart taste; eaten cooked or as a preserve.

stale breadcrumbs – crumbs made by grating, blending or processing 1- or 2-day-old bread.

SUGAR
brown – a very soft, fine sugar retaining molasses for its colour and flavour.
Caster – also known as superfine or finely granulated table sugar. Perfect for cakes, meringues and desserts.
icing – also known as confectioner's sugar.
white – granulated table sugar also known as crystal sugar

tartaric acid – used in making sweets and preserves; prevents the crystallisation of the sugar.

vanilla extract – obtained from vanilla beans infused in water; a non-alcoholic version of essence.

VINEGAR
cider – made from fermented apples.
malt – Made from a beer-like brew using malted barley.

195

glossary

INDEX

General Index

B
baking tips 143
Beer, Maggie 9, 16, 98, 130
Blanchett, Robyn 29, 123, 140
Burden, Hilary 159, 166
butter cakes, tips for baking 143

C
Clark, Pamela 73, 78, 120, 142–3, 181, 187
country-style cooking 8–9, 73

D
di Pieri, Stefano 9, 62, 91, 101, 108, 192
Dixon, Trisha 106, 148, 171

F
Flynn, Rachael 191

H
Hannemann, Jodi 86–7
homegrown produce 5, 16, 19, 71
Hughes, Tim 40, 69

I
Imhoff, Virginia 55, 182
ingenuity 8, 73

J
judging baked goods 142–3

K
Kelly, Jean 36, 156

L
Lonnie, Cathie 26
Lonnie, Wendy 92

M
MacTaggart, Claire 64, 133
Molesworth, Sal 49, 71

R
Royal Easter Show, Sydney 142–3

S
scones, tips for baking 143
shearers, cooking for 86–7
shearing schedules 87
Slack-Smith, Fiona 19, 111
sponges, tips for baking 143, 128

U
Underwood, Terry 5

W
Williams, Jenny 87

Recipe Index

A
anzac biscuits 34
apples
    apple and apricot jam 184
    crumble 167
    jelly 189
    old-fashioned apple pie 110
    sauce 95
spiced fig apple jam 183
apricots
    apple and apricot jam 184
    spiced apricot and plum pie 114

B
bananas
    banana and cinnamon muffins 31
    banana cake with passionfruit icing 141
beef
    beef and vegetable pie 105
    beef stew with parsley dumplings 157
    chunky beef and vegetable soup 149
    corned beef with parsley sauce 74
    curried sausages 162
    rissole, bacon and tomato casserole 162
    rissoles with grilled onions 67
    savoury-glazed meatloaf 70
    shepherd's pie 157
    standing rib roast with roast vegetables 105
    steak and kidney pie 150
berry frangipane tart 79
berry muffins 28
bircher muesli 14
biscuits see also cakes; muffins; rolls; slices
    anzac 34
    chocolate chip cookies 44
    gingernuts 47
    honey jumbles 38
    jam drops 47
    monte carlo 54
    rock cakes 43
    traditional shortbread 43
    vanilla kisses 37

bread and butter pudding 174
breakfasts
    banana and cinnamon muffins 31
    berry muffins 28
    bircher muesli 14
    cheese, corn and bacon muffins 31
    face at the window 25
    french toast 18
    overnight date and muesli muffins 28
    pancakes with lemon and sugar 18
    porridge 12
    roasted muesli with dried fruit and honey 14
    sauteed mushrooms 21
    scrambled eggs 25
    sunday fry-up 23
    butterscotch sauce 168

C
cakes see also biscuits; muffins; rolls; slices
    banana cake with passionfruit icing 141
    boiled chocolate 137
    carrot cake with lemon cream cheese frosting 141
    cinnamon teacake 138
    economical boiled fruit 129
    featherlight sponge 129
    hummingbird 126
    lamingtons 134
    orange 137
    patty cakes with glacé icing 132
    pink jelly cakes 135
    carrot cake with lemon cream cheese frosting 141
casseroles see stews/casseroles
cauliflower mornay 96
cheese béchamel 153
cheese, corn and bacon muffins 31
cheesecake, superb sour cream 85
chicken
    chicken and vegetable soup 90
    chicken liver pâté with port 63
    country-style terrine 64

INDEX

curried chicken pies 164
good old-fashioned chicken
   salad 67
roast chicken 99
chocolate
   boiled chocolate cake 137
   chocolate chip cookies 44
   chocolate self-saucing
      pudding 177
   hedgehog slice 125
chutney, spicy tomato 190
cinnamon teacake 138
citrus marmalade 184
college pudding 167
conserves see jam
cookies see biscuits
corned beef with parsley
   sauce 74
cream cheese topping 31
crumble, apple 167
curried chicken pies 164
curried sausages 162
custard 174
   baked 177

D

damper 76
dates
   date and walnut rolls 53
   overnight date and muesli
      muffins 28
   scones 57
   slice 121
   sticky date pudding with
      butterscotch sauce 168
desserts
   apple crumble 167
   baked custard 177
   berry frangipane tart 79
   bread and butter pudding 174
   chocolate self-saucing
      pudding 177
   classic trifle 82
   college pudding 167
   golden syrup dumplings 172
   impossible pie 85
   lemon delicious pudding 109
   lemon meringue pie 80
   old-fashioned apple pie 110
   passionfruit flummery 79
   pavlova 82
   rhubarb and pear sponge
      pudding 109
   rice pudding 113
   spiced apricot and plum pie 114
   steamed ginger pudding 113
   sticky date pudding with
      butterscotch sauce 168
   superb sour cream cheesecake 85
dijon vinaigrette 76
dutch ginger and almond slice 118

E

eggs
   face at the window 25
   french toast 18
   scrambled 25
   toasted ham sandwich with
      fried egg 153
   zucchini and mushroom
      omelette 21

F

fig jam and raisin rolls 50
frangipane 79
french toast 18
frosting see also icing
   cream cheese 126
   fudge 137
   lemon cream cheese 141
fruit cake, economical boiled 129
fudge frosting 137

G

garlic and rosemary smoked
   lamb 72
ginger
   dutch ginger and almond
      slice 118
   gingernuts 47
   grapefruit and ginger
      marmalade 180
   steamed ginger pudding 113
glacé icing 132
golden syrup dumplings 172
grapefruit and ginger
   marmalade 180

H

ham sandwich, toasted, with
   fried egg 153
hedgehog slice 125
herb stuffing 99
honey jumbles 38
hummingbird cake 126

I

icing 38, 134 see also frosting
   glacé 132
   passionfruit 110, 141
impossible pie 85

J

jam see also marmalade
   apple and apricot 184
   apple jelly 189
   dark plum 183
   jam drops 47
   jam roll 50
   peach and passionfruit 180
   quince jelly 189
   spiced fig apple 183
   strawberry conserve 184
jellies see jam

L

lamb
   barbecued lamb chops
      with mustard and
      thyme marinade 70
   garlic and rosemary smoked
      lamb 72
   lamb shank and vegetable
      soup 150
   lamb shank stew 102
   roast lamb dinner 96
   scotch broth 146
lamingtons 134
lemons
   lemon cream cheese frosting 141
   lemon delicious pudding 109
   lemon meringue pie 80
   tangy lemon squares 121

M

marmalade see also jam
   citrus 184
   grapefruit and ginger 180
mayonnaise 76
meatloaf, savoury-glazed 70
minestrone 149
mint sauce 96
monte carlo biscuits 54
mornay
   cauliflower 96
   tuna 160

INDEX

muesli
 bircher 14
 overnight date and muesli muffins 28
 roasted muesli with dried fruit and honey 14
muffins see also biscuits; cakes; rolls; slices
 banana and cinnamon 31
 berry 28
 cheese, corn and bacon 31
 overnight date and muesli 28
mushrooms, sauteed 21
mustard pickles, spicy 190

O
oak leaf and herb salad with dijon vinaigrette 76
omelettes see eggs
orange cake 137

P
pancakes with lemon and sugar 18
parsley dumplings 157
parsley sauce 74
passionfruit
 flummery 79
 icing 110, 141
 peach and passionfruit jam 180
pastry 80, 110
pâté, chicken liver with port 63
patties, salmon and potato 153
patty cakes with glacé icing 132
pavlova 82
peach and passionfruit jam 180
pies see also quiche lorraine
 beef and vegetable 105
 berry frangipane tart 79
 curried chicken 164
 impossible 85
 lemon meringue 80
 old-fashioned apple 110
 spiced apricot and plum pie 114
 steak and kidney 155
pikelets 37
plums
 dark plum jam 183
 spiced apricot and plum pie 114
pork
 country-style terrine 64
 grilled pork sausages with fruit relish 60
 pork leg roast with sage potatoes 94
porridge 12
potatoes
 potato and leek soup 93
 potato salad 76
 salmon and potato patties 153
pumpkin
 cream of pumpkin soup 93
 scones 57

Q
quiche lorraine 63
quince jelly 189

R
raspberry coconut slice 125
rhubarb and pear sponge pudding 109
rice pudding 113
rissole, bacon and tomato casserole 162
rissoles with grilled onions 67
rock cakes 43
rolls see also biscuits; cakes; muffins; slices
 date and walnut 53
 fig jam and raisin 50
 jam 50

S
salad
 good old-fashioned chicken 67
 oak leaf and herb salad with dijon vinaigrette 76
 potato 76
salmon and potato patties 153
sausages
 curried 162
 grilled pork sausages with fruit relish 60
scones
 basic 57
 date 57
 pumpkin 57
scotch broth 146
shepherd's pie 157
shortbread, traditional 43
slices see also biscuits; cakes; muffins; rolls
 date 121
 dutch ginger and almond 118
 hedgehog 125
 raspberry coconut 125
 tangy lemon squares 121
soups
 chicken and vegetable 90
 chunky beef and vegetable 149
 cream of pumpkin 93
 lamb shank and vegetable 150
 minestrone 149
 potato and leek 93
 scotch broth 146
spiced apricot and plum pie 114
spiced fig apple jam 183
spiced yogurt cream 114
spicy mustard pickles 190
spicy tomato chutney 190
sponge cake, featherlight 129
steak and kidney pie 155
stews/casseroles
 beef stew with parsley dumplings 157
 lamb shank stew 102
 rissole, bacon and tomato casserole 162
strawberry conserve 184
sunday fry-up 23

T
tarts see pies
terrine, country-style 64
tomato chutney, spicy 190
trifle, classic 82
tuna mornay 160

V
vanilla kisses 37
vegetables, roasted root 99
vienna cream 37, 54

Z
zucchini and mushroom omelette 21

CONVERSION CHART

MEASURES

One Australian metric measuring cup holds approximately 250ml; one Australian metric tablespoon holds 20ml; one Australian metric teaspoon holds 5ml.

The difference between one country's measuring cups and another's is within a two- or three-teaspoon variance, and will not affect your cooking results. North America, New Zealand and the United Kingdom use a 15ml tablespoon.

All cup and spoon measurements are level. The most accurate way of measuring dry ingredients is to weigh them. When measuring liquids, use a clear glass or plastic jug with the metric markings.

We use large eggs with an average weight of 60g.

DRY MEASURES

METRIC	IMPERIAL
15g	½oz
30g	1oz
60g	2oz
90g	3oz
125g	4oz (¼lb)
155g	5oz
185g	6oz
220g	7oz
250g	8oz (½lb)
280g	9oz
315g	10oz
345g	11oz
375g	12oz (¾lb)
410g	13oz
440g	14oz
470g	15oz
500g	16oz (1lb)
750g	24oz (1½lb)
1kg	32oz (2lb)

LIQUID MEASURES

METRIC	IMPERIAL
30ml	1 fluid oz
60ml	2 fluid oz
100ml	3 fluid oz
125ml	4 fluid oz
150ml	5 fluid oz (¼ pint/1 gill)
190ml	6 fluid oz
250ml	8 fluid oz
300ml	10 fluid oz (½ pint)
500ml	16 fluid oz
600ml	20 fluid oz (1 pint)
1000ml (1 litre)	1¾ pints

LENGTH MEASURES

METRIC	IMPERIAL
3mm	⅛ in
6mm	¼in
1cm	½in
2cm	¾in
2.5cm	1in
5cm	2in
6cm	2½in
8cm	3in
10cm	4in
13cm	5in
15cm	6in
18cm	7in
20cm	8in
23cm	9in
25cm	10in
28cm	11in
30cm	12in (1ft)

OVEN TEMPERATURES

These oven temperatures are only a guide for conventional ovens. For fan-forced ovens, check the manufacturer's manual.

	°C (CELSIUS)	°F (FAHRENHEIT)	GAS MARK
Very slow	120	250	½
Slow	150	275-300	1-2
Moderately slow	160	325	3
Moderate	180	350-375	4-5
Moderately hot	200	400	6
Hot	220	425-450	7-8
Very hot	240	475	9

General manager Christine Whiston
Editorial director Susan Tomnay
Creative director Hieu Chi Nguyen
Managing editor Elizabeth Wilson
Art director & designer Hannah Blackmore
Senior editor Stephanie Kistner
Food director Pamela Clark
Food editor Cathie Lonnie

Photographers Chris Chen, Louise Lister, Andre Martin, Rob Palmer, George Seper, Brett Stevens, John Paul Urizar, Ian Wallace, Gorta Yuuki, Tanya Zouev
Stylists Kristen Beusing, Alexia Biggs, Margot Braddon, Kirsty Cassidy, Marie-Helene Clauzon, Jane Hann, Michaela Le Compte, Vicki Liley, Sarah O'Brien, Louise Pickford, Stephanie Souvlis

Additional photography George Seper, David Hahn
Additional styling Alexia Biggs
Food preparation Angela Muscat

Director of sales Brian Cearnes
Marketing manager Bridget Cody
Marketing & promotions assistant Xanthe Roberts
Senior business analyst Rebecca Varela
Operations manager David Scotto
Production manager Victoria Jefferys
European rights enquiries Laura Bamford
lbamford@acpuk.com

ACP Books are published by ACP Magazines
a division of PBL Media Pty Limited
Publishing director, Women's lifestyle Pat Ingram
Director of sales, Women's lifestyle Lynette Phillips
Commercial manager, Women's lifestyle Seymour Cohen
Marketing director, Women's lifestyle
Matthew Dominello
Public relations manager, Women's lifestyle
Hannah Deveraux
Research Director, Women's lifestyle Justin Stone
PBL Media, Chief Executive Officer Ian Law

The publishers would like to thank the following people for locations used in photography:
Michelle Cambridge from The Shady Fig, Nowra, NSW
Mark Starling from Blackdown Estate, Bathurst, NSW and Richard and Lucy Marshall at Merribee, Numbaa, NSW
And the following businesses for providing props used in photography:
David Jones, Donaldson Enterprises, Doug Up on Bourke, Honeybee Homewares, No Chintz, Royal Doulton and The Bay Tree.

Produced by ACP Books, Sydney.
Published by ACP Books, a division of ACP Magazines Ltd.
54 Park St, Sydney NSW Australia 2000.
GPO Box 4088, Sydney, NSW 2001.
Phone +61 2 9282 8618 Fax +61 2 9267 9438
acpbooks@acpmagazines.com.au www.acpbooks.com.au
Printed by C&C Offset Printing, China.
Australia Distributed by Network Services,
GPO Box 4088, Sydney, NSW 2001.
Phone +61 2 9282 8777 Fax +61 2 9264 3278
networkweb@networkservicescompany.com.au
United Kingdom Distributed by Australian Consolidated Press (UK),
10 Scirocco Close, Moulton Park Office Village, Northampton, NN3 6AP.
Phone +44 1604 642 200 Fax +44 1604 642 300
books@acpuk.com www.acpuk.com
New Zealand Distributed by Southern Publishers Group,
21 Newton Road, Newton, Auckland.
Phone +64 9 360 0692 Fax +64 9 360 0695 hub@spg.co.nz
South Africa Distributed by PSD Promotions,
30 Diesel Road Isando, Gauteng Johannesburg.
PO Box 1175, Isando 1600, Gauteng Johannesburg.
Phone +27 11 392 6065/6/7 Fax +27 11 392 6079/80
orders@psdprom.co.za
Canada Distributed by Publishers Group Canada
Order Desk & Customer Service:
9050 Shaughnessy Street, Vancouver, BC V6P 6E5
Phone (800) 663 5714 Fax (800) 565 3770 service@raincoast.com

Title: The Country Table.
Publisher: ACP Books.
ISBN: 978-1-86396-872-0
Notes: Includes index.
Subjects: Cookery (natural foods)
Dewey Number: 641.5
Copyright © ACP Magazines Ltd 2009
ABN 18 053 273 546

This publication is copyright. No part of it may be reproduced or transmitted in any form without the written permission of the publishers.

To order books, phone 136 116 (within Australia) or
online at www.magshop.com.au
Send recipe enquiries to: recipeenquiries@acpmagazines.com.au